WITHDRAWN FROM STOCK

THE FORESTS OF ENGLAND

Also by Peter J. Neville Havins

Portrait of Worcestershire

The Spas of England

The Matchbox (poetry)

The Short Life and Small Times of Bingo Disco (play)

THE FORESTS OF ENGLAND

Peter J. Neville Havins

LONDON
ROBERT HALE & COMPANY

First published in Great Britain 1976

ISBN 0 7091. 5469 0

Robert Hale & Company
Clerkenwell House
Clerkenwell Green
London EC1R 0HT

Filmset by Specialised Offset Services Limited, Liverpool
and printed in Great Britain by
Lowe & Brydone Limited
Thetford, Norfolk

CONTENTS

ILLUSTRATIONS

PICTURE CREDITS

Colin and Janet Bord, 1, 2, 3, 9, 20; Derek Widdicombe, 4; J. Allan Cash Ltd., 5, 6, 11, 12, 28; Anthony Brown, 7; Thomas A. Wilkie, 8, 14, 16, 19, 26, 29, 30; John Markham, 10; Roy A. Harris and K.R. Duff, 13, 15, 27; Radio Times Hulton Picture Library, 17, 18, 21, 22, 23, 24; Geoffrey Wright, 25.

Dedicated to

Tracy, Michael and Paul
and the memory of
a now defunct 'Beetle' registration number FEC 321
without whose efforts most of this book would not
have been possible

1

The Well Wooded Country

Any consideration of England's surviving forest areas almost inevitably brings a few well-known names to mind, such as Sherwood, Epping, the Forest of Dean, the New Forest and perhaps even the non-woodland area of the Forest of Arden. But, in distant times, these now largely preserved areas of woodland would have formed indistinguishable parts of the vast tract of forest which covered most of England's lowland regions. The domestic, industrial and other needs of an ever increasing population have, over the centuries, at first slowly but later with increasing rapidity all but denuded this once greatly afforested country. The history of England's forest land is, until comparatively recent times, greatly a record of the continual shrinkage of native timber resources.

The extent of afforestation in times immediately prior to the Roman occupation can only be arrived at by intelligent guesswork. However, the communications system developed by the late Iron-Age Celtic population gives a reasonably good indication of some more general limits. Forts and settlements of the Iron-Age period tended to be built on high ground; this tendency can be only partially accounted for by the military consideration of a defensive position, for though the Iron-Age Celts did occasionally wage war against each other they were, in the years immediately preceding the Roman invasion, a relatively stable society, split into a number of independent kingdoms some of which had sufficiently developed to possess their own currency.

The main reason for the Celtic preoccupation with high ground was quite simple. Much of the lowland was forest, not well-tended forest land such as that which we are nowadays accustomed to find in such places as the Forest of Dean, but vast, tangled, impenetrable woodland. This not merely overlay the lowland areas but, in many cases, literally choked them with a seemingly endless growth whose density it is now difficult to imagine. Forest on such a scale was, for the Celts, an insurmountable barrier. Clearings were made upon its fringes but no one ventured to carve through it and it was left as the largely undisturbed home of such animals as the wolf and wild boar. Even when the Roman legions began their conquering drives into the west and north they tended to construct their roads so that they skirted the major areas of forest and, as was the case with the Fosse Way, followed the lines of existing ridgeway tracks.

When the high land civilization of the Iron-Age Celts, symbolized by such high ground sites as Stonehenge, Avebury and Rollright and by camps ranging from Dorset's Maiden Castle to those of Malvern and Shropshire's Caer Caradoc, fell to the Romans, it was a superimposed lowland civilization which took its place.

Yet even the Romans were not to make much of an impression on the forests of their new province of Brittannia. However, it would be true to say that they made the first organized and extensive use of local timber partly for domestic and other building, partly for shipbuilding and partly for industrial use. It was the Roman extension of the salt industry based on what was later to be known as Droitwich that began the process that was eventually to lead to the complete denudation of the forests of Feckenham and Horewell and it was the needs of the same industry that began to bite into the woodland later to be known as the Forest of Delamere around Nantwich. Some of their new roads also necessitated clearing ways through the woodland but, by the time the Romans – or rather the motley racial collection that made up the imperial army – left, it would be true to say that they had done little more than tinker with the primaeval structure of most of the local topography.

It is strange to realize that when the advance guard of the various races which were later destined to fuse into the English nation first arrived upon the shores of this island there were still large parts of it which had never known the foot of man. But it was hardly this area in which the new, conquering settlers were interested. Once they had begun to drive back the Romanized Celtic population they were soon to turn their hands to farming and it was only when existing agricultural land began to give out in relation to the increasing number of settlers that incursions began to be made into the forest.

It was the pressure and needs of an expanding Anglo-Saxon population which occasioned the first major inroads into the native woodland. Unlike the Romano-Celts whom they surplanted over most of the country, the new settlers showed little desire to make use of earlier Roman sites of buildings. There were to be some exceptions to this, as at London, York and perhaps Chester, but in general the Saxons were disinclined to accept a Roman heritage. There were many reasons for this, perhaps a major one being the natural disdain of aggressive conquerors for the creations of the vanquished. To live with the symbols of this fallen civilization was also probably considered by a supersitious people to be courting some form of divine retribution. Again, by the very fact that they had fallen before them, the Saxons must have considered the Roman sites indefensible and, rather than attempt to remedy the defect, preferred to build defensive sites of their own. These were the burghs, defensive earthworks with ditches and palisades such as that originally thrown up around the Wessex capital of Winchester. Walls came later when, paradoxically, society was more stable and the need for defence was not so great.

Unlike the Romans, the early Saxons had no tradition of architecture which went beyond that of essentially small scale utility. Because their society was based on local groupings rather than as a nation they originally had no tradition of civic architecture either. Theirs was not the world of the Forum, the Principia, of aqueducts, ampitheatres, villas and hypocausts. Theirs was the world of the settlement and of its defensive guarantee, the war-band. Architecturally this was the world of the small-holding and – as the war-bands ceased to rove and plunder westward and to become increasingly established on the land – of the moothall where, in a theoretically free assembly of equals, all could raise matters of local dispute. Even with the coming of the Church and with the slow evolution of townships this was hardly a society that could be expected to be marked by significant architectural achievement. Partly as a result of this most Saxon building tended to be of timber, something which accounts for so little of it surviving into our own times. It is, however, possible to trace the lines of some Anglo-Saxon buildings, notably churches, because their later stone replacements stuck closely to an existing ground-plan.

This Saxon preoccupation with timber for domestic and other building, while it did not place a great strain on the woodlands, can hardly have been without its effects. Nor can the ceaseless demand for fuel, for the use of coal was to remain slight until the end of medieval times. Fuel was required not only for domestic purposes but for the growing needs of an itinerant metal industry, especially in the regions of the Weald and the Forest of Dean. Legend has it that in the Mercian heart of the country, the smiths of Alcester required so much timber for their forges that they were responsible for much of the denudation of the Forest of Arden. There is probably very little factual basis to this particular legend which may have had as its roots an attempt to explain the existence of the ruins of the Roman town. But, in this case, it was quite literally probably a case of there being no smoke without fire and points to the existence of iron-working here at least as early as the eighth century.

Iron working had been taking place in Britain since long before the Roman invasion and one of the things that had first brought the Celtic inhabitants to Roman notice was the habit of some southern tribes of using iron bars as their basic currency. Given the scarcity value of the metal in the Roman world this was not unlike the sixteenth-century fables of the inhabitants of Eldorado using gold for their pots and pans. The bronze and various Iron Ages have not been so called for nothing and Britain's later inhabitants only extended what had been long begun. Someone at least had to make horseshoes and, amongst other things, they also had to make cooking vessels and weapons as well.

But one thing that the early Saxons do not appear to have shared with their Celtic predecessors was the veneration of the tree. True, Saxon and Norse religion had the Tree of Life as the centre of creation. But it would be true to say that it was hardly a tree destined to sink very deep roots on these shores. On the other hand, certain species of tree had an important relevance to Celtic religion. The Druids had their sacred groves, sacred oaks and, of course, mistletoe. Just what were the exact elements that composed the druidical religion we cannot be sure. Yet, even after the coming of the Saxons and later of the Church, its remnants lingered in the fringes of the minds of the Celtic population, especially in the racial redoubts that some of the forest areas became. It is a mistake to assume that the invading Saxons hit these shores in invincible waves, subduing all before them and driving the Celtic population ever further and further westward. The Saxon conquest was a long drawn out and piecemeal affair and one thing they could not subdue was the forest. Even if they had wanted to keep ahead of the advancing invaders many Celts were probably unable to do so and would have become trapped in the woodland depths as the Saxons swept by to occupy the more open land surrounding them.

In time an uneasy co-existence would have developed and in the woodland the old religion would have lingered. When the Church came to mount its onslaught on the shadowy mythology of the Saxons it was to succeed well enough – but it, too, was to find the forests almost impenetrable. Here it was not the worship of Thor and Woden which survived but a debased form of the old druidical cults, the remnants of which in later years were to be collectively termed witchcraft. Some of the ancient practices were destined to survive when they became associated with aspects of later folklore. In many forest areas what had originally been fertility dances came to be performed by groups of men such as the band known as Robin Hood's Men who would dance their way around Chaddesley Corbbett and other villages in the Feckenham Forest region. Today one of the few surviving memorials of those times is to be found in the horn-dance at Staffordshire's Abbott's Bromley.

But although the Saxons and the surviving Celtic inhabitants were to make some inroads into the forest areas – ample evidence of this is to be found in placenames, especially those ending in 'ley' or 'hay', both words originally signifying a clearing – the country was still dominantly forest at the time of the Norman invasion. In fact much forest land remained uncharted and ill-defined and was not considered as a part of the kingdom at all. Large areas were simply described as "Nanesmansland", in which the royal writ did not run and over which the king claimed no jurisdiction. This was 'the waste', trackless forest and moor, almost entirely abandoned to wild animals and with a minimal population which royal officials at least did not think were worth bothering about. The Norman concept of the royal forest had yet to find expression in England, though Edward the Confessor was to make provisions for the royal parks to be policed by wardens and earlier Cnut was to enact some fairly stringent forest laws. But, in general, the Saxons were concerned only with those areas of woodland that were of immediate use to them – with, for example, the Weald and Forests of Delamere and Feckenham because they provided for the needs of relatively long-established industry, with Ytene – later to be known as the New Forest – because it provided material for the building of England's navy. It was largely to be left to the Norman invaders to incorporate the sprawling forest wastes into the land they conquered.

Yet the Normans did not precipitate complete change in the English woodlands. Although the Anglo-Saxons had a considerably different administrative style than that to be practised by their Norman successors, by the end of what could perhaps be called the most truly English period of English history, the general pattern of woodland activity, as it was to continue and expand through the remaining Middle Ages, was already largely established.

Although many regions were officially classed as waste and regarded as uninhabited the forests, in fact, had their charcoal-burners – the original colliers – and woodsmen. Their names were destined to outlive the medieval period in surnames such as Cole, Wood, Sawyer, Attwood and so forth. Some, such as the royal parks and Church lands – as in that around the ancient capital of Winchester – had their local officials, the forerunners of the woodwards, agisters, haywards and verderers of Norman times. Apart from charcoal burning, many of the trades to be so long associated with the forests were already long-established, especially the shipbuilding of the south and the itinerant metal industry of the Weald and Forest of Dean.

Slow though the process may appear to us now the area of actual woodland was continually contracting and it was to be the Normans who were first to attempt to check the movement, although official efforts at reafforestation still lay many centuries ahead. But it was neither the needs of industry nor of large-scale building that was the dominant cause of this. The reason is to be found in the growing scarcity of easily worked agricultural land. Anglo-Saxon England had ceased to be a pioneering society and the Saxons would hardly have bothered to carve their way into the forests at all if they could have found good land without such trouble – but they could not. The dispossessed Celts had been pushed back to the western highlands, the downs and open heathlands were largely infertile areas and if the Saxons wanted anything like a return for their husbandry they had to hack clearings in the forest.

Even the needs of one Saxon small-holder could effect a considerable change in land usage. He had to clear enough land to enable him to make at least a bare living, to provide for the shelter of his family and stock and for the making of many of his implements, for even such things as ploughs and spades were made of wood. In fact the only thing that the Anglo-Saxon smallholder did not make from wood or obtain from the forge of the local smith was his millstone – a fact which early tended to set the miller apart from the rest of the agricultural community. Above all the smallholder required fuel, something which imposed a continual drain on the surrounding woodland. When an original clearing came in time to be occupied by a group of farmers – became not just a 'ley' but a 'ham' – it is not hard to see that before long a large area of forest would disappear.

If would, however, be a mistake to suppose that, by the mid eleventh century, Anglo-Saxon England was still the same primitive landholding society it had been four centuries earlier. Late Anglo-Saxon society was remarkably sophisticated. It was certainly very much more sophisticated than the dukedoms of Normandy, Brittany and Flanders from where most of its conquerors were soon destined to come.

Although the major earldoms of Wessex, Mercia and Northumbria still remained powerful, England had long ago moved toward a centralized system of government, though this was somewhat complicated by London rising as the kingdom's commercial capital while Winchester remained the main seat of royal administration and the Treasury. Nevertheless, Anglo-Saxon government contained the nucleus of a representative system in the Witan. By contrast the early Norman system of government was that of military despotism.

The artistic trappings of the court remained some of the most impressive in Western Europe, and England led the world in metal-working and in the medieval art of illumination. On a more far-reaching level, industry, although necessarily on a small scale, was growing and apart from the iron and other metal trades, included tanning, brewing, ceramics, dying and shipbuilding, although husbandry in all its forms engaged the vast majority of the population. Compared to the state of political affairs in most of Europe, England was an enormous area to be under one administration. Forests and wasteland not withstanding, it was a considerable achievement that the English had brought about before the Norman warlords landed on the Sussex coast.

2

The Laws of the Forest

It was that Al Capone of English history, William the Conqueror, who very largely established what could be called the equestrian concepts of 'the forest'. This could have been defined as applying to an area of land, usually largely wooded though not necessarily so, in which the leading representative of a collection of generally illiterate opportunist thugs – sometimes described by later historians as the Norman aristocracy – enjoyed exclusive privilege of the chase. In return the animals were protected from all but regal interference with their cover. Before this the English, if they had known of the word, would probably have referred to most later royal forest areas not as waste, nor even as Nanesmansland, but as jungle.

As already mentioned in the previous chapter there had been some movement toward royal control of certain forest areas – largely in the south – in the decades immediately prior to the Norman invasion. This extension of royal control had been made not only by Edward the Confessor but by another conquering warrior king, Cnut, who had briefly reforged England's link with its northern past and made it part of his Scandanavian Empire. Cnut had early recognized the right of his noblemen – his axe-honing collection of jarls and stallers – to hunt the game in their own preserves and had issued a stern warning urging his subjects to refrain from interference with the royal hunt: "let everyone abstain from my hunting on pain of the full fine, take heed where I will have no trespassing on my hunting".

A few people may have found themselves virtually bankrupted as a result of this – but Cnut's warning was the voice of moderation compared to what was to happen under William. It was to Cnut's proclamation that William was to look when first framing the original Laws of the Forest. He was quite determined to put the new laws into effect but, not wishing to alienate his English subjects completely, sought to shift the onus for their existence to the Carta Canuti, a document supposedly unearthed at Winchester. It was from this, and not from William himself, that the new king maintained the Forest Laws originated – all he was doing, so he said, was codifying them. It must be said that William's claim was generally disbelieved and, from contemporary accounts, certainly the representatives of the Church were far from convinced. In the matter of the Forest Laws, as in most things in England, William got his way largely because he governed as a military dictator.

But William's concern with the forests was not solely related to the pleasures of the chase. One reason for the existence of so much 'waste' in eleventh-century England was because the country was, compared to much of Western Europe, underpopulated. Clearings had been made in the forest, some small settlements had grown up and industry and domestic needs had caused some diminution of its original extent. Yet all this constituted little more than a series of pin-pricks, judged by the fact that Nanesmansland was not so much a description of wilderness as an expression of official disinterest with regions of very low population.

The Saxon administration may have felt it could well afford to ignore these areas; but William and his henchmen could not. The Norman administration had to bring all areas of the country within its control, for there was every danger that resistence would linger and possibly grow in these inaccessible regions. Though other reasons and causes have been advanced it was partly in an effort to stave off insurrection that William's Forest Laws were so framed that initially they led to a shinkage of the forest population and a number of forest villages ceased to exist. The conquerors obviously considered that they could only trust their subjects as far as they could see them.

William's Forest Laws were patterned upon those established by the Carolingian emperors and were of a severity previously unknown in England. No copy of William's original laws has survived and the earliest example we have of the Forest Law of Norman times is the Assize of the Forest of 1184 made in the reign of Henry II. This, however, was probably little more than a re-enactment of earlier Forest Law and gives a good indication of what William's own laws were like.

The formulation of the Forest Law also lead to the complimentary creation of a mass of officials to administer it. The major royal official in any area officially classed as royal forest was the master forester sometimes, as in the Forest of Feckenham, called the Warden or, as in the case of the Forest of Dean, the Constable, who was in fact the Constable of St Briavel's Castle, responsible for royal administration in the Hundred of St Braivel's which was roughly co-extensive with the forest. Beneath the master forester came the sub-foresters, or foresters-in-fee who were responsible for the implementation of his orders on such matters as the provision of timber for royal needs. Also beneath the master forester were the verderers, legal officials who dealt with offences against the animals or cover in the vederers' court or the court of swanimote. Beneath the sub-foresters were the officials known as woodwards or haywards, who were really gamekeepers, while the last in line were the agisters who were basically rent-collectors employed by the verderers to collect fees due for the use of forest land for authorized grazing and pasture.

In time this chain of royal officialdom came to be generally hated, not only by the commoners who could hardly help brushing against it from time to time, but by both the baronage and the Church. William was to extend the royal forest far beyond his own Crown land to cover those which were in the hands of barons and churchmen and many of these found it distasteful to obey a law which occasionally gave them, by way of a special dispensation, only the rights of warren – the chase of the fox, hare, pheasant, partridge and so on – but reserved to the king alone the chase of the deer and wild boar. Whenever the medieval monarchy showed signs of weakness the king's rights under Forest Law were always to figure amongst the major grievances put forward by his opponents.

Perhaps the most well-known of William's applications of

Forest Law was in respect of the former waste of Ytene which was now to be restyled the New Forest. But there were other areas where Forest Law was to be applied with equal ferocity and he was to include almost the whole of Essex as well as large parts of Sussex, Hertfordshire and Worcestershire as well. Ytene, was originally more heath and scrubland than wooded forest and here the Norman administration created the New Forest by considerably enlarging the area of forest administration.

The Doomsday Survey shows that thirty manors in the region had gone out of cultivation since the time of the Conquest and though some of these may have done so through natural reasons – much of the land was not very fertile – it is quite probable that others were depopulated as being settlements in infringement of the new laws. In the New Forest few landholders were exempt from the operation of the laws – the Abbots of Beaulieu being amongst the few exceptions. Lyndhurst was the capital of forest administration where there still stands the later Verderer's Hall and, within it, the symbolic reminder of forest law, the stirrup through which all dogs kept in the forest had to pass if they were to escape lawing. This was the removal of the three claws from the forefeet to prevent dogs being used for hunting. But, even in the New Forest, the Norman record was not entirely a bad one and at least they provided it with a scattering of churches, including that at Boldre. The reason for the forest's popularity with the early Norman kings lay in the fact that it stood near the southern centres of administration, Winchester and London. The Norman monarchs, with their interests in their own duchy and in continual dispute with the kings of France were, like the Romans before them, not unnaturally biased toward the English south and bequeathed to English government a preoccupation with the area that has yet to desert it.

The native English regarded William's preoccupation with the forest and chase as a perverse eccentricity and the anonymous, but presumably Saxon author of the Peterborough version of the *Anglo Saxon Chronicle*, in summing up William's reign upon his death in 1087, concludes on a note of wonderment, that "he preserved the harts and boars and loved the stags as much as if he had been their father". The English, and very possibly some of the Anglo-Norman war-lords who very quickly came to identify themselves with their new territories, were hopeful that William's successors would show less enthusiasm for the chase. But this was wishful thinking. Succeeding Norman and Angevin monarchs were to retain at least those areas where Forest Law had operated in William's reign and in some cases to extend it. Churchmen, Norman as well as English, were particularly angered by the laws applying in places which they contended had been given to the Church alone; and they regarded their administration by officials over whom they had no control as an injustifiable intrusion into the rights of the Church. Although this was only one element in the Church-and-State battle for political supremacy that occupied the eleventh, twelfth and thirteenth centuries it was undoubtably a factor in leading to the probable clerical conspiracy which resulted in the mysterious New Forest death of William Rufus.

In point of fact William Rufus did not make any great additions to the extent of forest land but his brother and successor, Henry I, did. When Henry's death produced the civil war of Stephen and Matilda, Stephen attempted to win support from Church and baronage by promising to do away with Henry's additions. In 1136 he undertook to "restore and surrender to the churches and the kingdom" Henry's extensions of the forest and "reserve for my own use" only these forest areas "which William, my grandfather, and William, my uncle, established and maintained". But, even judged by medieval standards, Stephen's reign was something of an aberation and when strong monarchy was restored under Henry II the new king, far from honouring Stephen's promises, he made even greater extensions to the regions under forest law.

By the end of Henry II's reign the forest laws were being administered over roughly a third of the kingdom and had reached the widest extent of their application. Henry was one of England's strongest medieval monarchs and the wide bounds of the forest were an expression of this power. But Henry's enormous Continental holdings were both his power and his weakness. Under his sons Richard and John the

Angevin inheritance crumbled to the point where England was subject to a French invasion. Both were forced to sell off forest land to meet their expenses – and in the case of John, to dilute forest law as part of the price of baronial support. Though the early Plantagenat kings were to re-assert some of their former forest rights, royal power in the forests was henceforth to be in steady retreat.

Yet this whittling down of the power of an oppressive monarchy was a process which took many years and the punishments meted out for infringements of the forest laws could still be barbarous. For offences against the forest laws a man could 'answer with his body' – a phrase which could encompass hanging and such mutilations as castration and blinding. Whole villages were often fined as a penalty for the unexplained disappearance of deer. As the author of the twelfth-century *Dialogue of the Exchequer* said, forest law was not common law but "the will and whim of the king. So that whatever has been done according to it may be said to be not absolutely just, but just according to the law of the forest."

The churchmen were especially opposed to it because it expressly denied them benefit of clergy – the right of a cleric to be tried for an offence not in the secular courts but in the court of the local bishop. It was also the operation of the forest laws which tended to turn a great number of England's rural population into outlaws – something which was almost inevitable considering its far-reaching application and its severity. While most people lived under common law – a system which had its roots deep in the Anglo Saxon past – forest dwellers lived under what they rightly considered the harsh despotism of an alien administration. It is hardly surprising, therefore, that the outlaw legends come almost exclusively from the forest law areas where the Robin Hood-like fight against tyranny and injustice had its roots in a very real situation.

Some extracts from Henry II's Assize of the forest – the earliest example that exists of the forest laws – gives a fair indication of the laws as they had been in operation over the first century of Norman rule. The Assize was first published at Woodstock, a particularly appropriate place as this was the location of the king's major hunting lodge in the Midland shires.

This is the English assize of the Lord King Henry, son of Matilda, which he has made for the protection of his forests and forest game, with the advice and approval of the archbishops and bishops, and of the barons, earls, and nobles of England, at Woodstock.

1. To begin with, he forbids anyone to offend against him in any particular touching his forests or his forest game; and he desires that no one shall place confidence in the fact that he has hitherto been moderate in his punishment of offenders against his forests and his forest game, and has taken from them only their chattels in satisfaction for their offences. For if anyone offends against him in future and is convicted for his offence, the king will have from him the full measure of justice which was exacted in the time of King Henry, his grandfather.

2. He forbids that anyone shall have bows, arrows, hounds or harriers in his forests, except by license from the king or other duly authorized person.

3. He forbids any owner of a wood within King Henry's forest to sell or give away anything out of the wood to its wasting or destruction: but he allows that they may take freely from their woods to satisfy their own needs, provided they do so without wasting, and under the supervision of the king's forester.

4. The king has commanded that where any of the demesne woods of the lord king are destroyed and the forester in charge of them is unable to account satisfactorily for their destruction, he shall not be fined, but shall answer with his own body.

5. The king forbids any clerk in holy oders to offend against him in respect of his forests or of his forest game. He has given strict instructions to his foresters that they shall not hesitate to lay hands upon such persons, if they find them offending, in order to restrain them and secure their arrest; and he will cover them fully in his actions by his personal warrant.

12. At Woodstock, the king commanded that for a first and second offence a man shall give safe pledges (for future good behaviour) but that for a third offence no further pledges shall be taken from him, nor shall he be allowed any other measure of satisfaction, but he shall answer with his own body.

13. The king commands that all males over the age of twelve years who live in an area where game is protected shall take an oath for the protection of the game. Clerks in holy orders with lay

holdings within the area shall not be exempt from taking the oath.

14. The king commands that wherever his wild animals are protected, or have customarily enjoyed protection, mastiffs shall be lawed.

15. The king absolutely forbids that in future anyone shall hunt wild animals by night, with a view to their capture, in areas where his wild animals are protected or outside these areas in places where they are often to be found or where protection was formerly applied, on penalty of one year's imprisonment or the payment of a fine and ransom this same penalty, shall set traps for the king's wild animals, using dead or live animals as bait, anywhere within the king's forests and woods, or within areas which used to form part of a forest, but were later disafforested by the king or his progenitors.

For many centuries the chief offenders against the forest laws would appear to have been those same officials whose duty it was to enforce them. This disease of maladministration applied, to some degree, to all forest land, where the most important local officials were often the relatives of local landowners. At a local level medieval justice was very often a family matter and well-placed lawbreakers could often ensure that they got away with only minimal punishment or, far more likely, with no punishment at all.

Various monarchs may have attempted to enforce stringest measures – but they were very largely powerless against their subversion by their own officials. Two cases from the thirteenth-century administration of Feckenham Forest may serve as examples. In 1270 Richard of Montrivon, forester-in-fee for the bailiwick of Popperode – near Alcester – and the royal enclosure of Lickey, was deproved of his lands and office for "laying waste timber" under his care. He was also accused of having bribed three under-foresters and two officials known as 'tunwards' to join him. Nevertheless, for the payment of a small fine, Richard was given back his lands and office and presumably things went on much as before. Ten years later, at the Forest Court of Feckenham, Adam le Bold, was fined 100 marks for "making and permitting waste". This Adam was no mere forester-in-fee but the actual Warden of the Forest, the chief cog in the machine of local forest-law administration.

Far from protecting the royal interests he had done the exact reverse. He was accused not only of making a handsome profit by having timber felled and sold illegally but also of appointing as gamekeepers men who were well-known as professional poachers. In fact, Adam had put most of the administrative posts up for sale to the highest bidder and had netted a fat profit as a result. Other officials, at various times, were accused of much the same sort of thing. Some were alleged to have given landowners 'permission' – for a payment, of course – to extend their holdings by the cultivation of forest land. Nor do they seem to have been above embezzling money taken in fines in the forest courts. A few did pay for their actions, but more got away with them, while the majority of those brought to book managed to avoid the full legal consequences. Given such a situation it is hardly surprising that the monarchy found its forests shrinking from within.

That the forest officials were occasionally subject to punishment was not normally due to the processes of the local forest courts but to the courts of the king's forest justices-in-eyre. Henry II appointed one chief justice of the forest to hear the more important cases and later Henry II appointed two, one to be responsible for the forests south of the Trent, the other for those north of the Trent. Other judges often sat with the forest justices and heard evidence brought before them by the regarders, the twelve knights of each forest area charged with making a pre-eyre survey of the forest and its administration. It was this evidence which the forest officials themselves often had to answer. The forest justices also heard the more serious cases brought before the court by the master forester and the verderers.

Once these courts were established the major punishments of death and mutilation came to be almost solely reserved to them. Yet, by the time they were set up, the gory days of official mayhem had almost ended in the forest lands. This was not due to humanitarian considerations but to economic ones. England's kings tended to be both ambitious and short of money and a large contribution to the royal coffers in the form of a substantial fine was far more welcome than a severed hand. Of course, if an offender was himself without financial resource then a head or some form of mutilation had to suffice. But it he could pay then pay he did.

In fact, by the end of the thirteenth century, the forest lands had become almost indispensible sources of royal revenue. The royal game was now, if not exactly irrelevant, certainly far less important than the fines, rents and fees which annually went to swell the royal treasury. It was very much because of this that England's later medieval kings hung onto the royal forests with such tenacity. Game was a side-issue; but the forest laws spelt money.

But if the kings enjoyed receiving the revenue from forest law fines then the offenders brooked at providing it. In this context it would be wrong to think that the forest laws marred only the existence of the poorer folk. True they pressed on these most hard for the laws often struck at the very roots of their livelihood. But, though the local forest courts were full of erring peasantry, it was the barons and churchmen who contributed the bulk of the fines. What really angered the landowners and prelates was that they were often fined for hunting over their own land for, when this came within the boundary of the Royal Forest, though they might enjoy the privilege of warren, they rarely had the right to hunt the stag, deer and wild boar. As far as they were concerned the Laws of the Forest were an unjust infringement of their personal liberties.

For long the commoners had no real means of voicing their grievances, but the barons and churchmen had. Whenever the king got himself into a particularly difficult situation and needed finance for a foreign war or to put down an internal rebellion, barons and churchmen would unite to wring what concessions they could as a prerequisite for their co-operation. This may have been odious for the king but then, given the chance, he behaved odiously toward everyone else. High on the list of such concessions were generally demands that the extent of the area over which Forest Law applied be diminished and that where it was retained, its operation be made less drastic.

John was the first English monarch to become seriously embroiled with his own barons and churchmen. After losing Normandy and having England invaded by the pursuing

French, John was so hard pressed that he signed Magna Carta. In popular mythology 1215 is the year when Englishmen reclaimed their ancient liberties. In actual fact it was merely one more time when the baronage – of both the sacred and the profane brands – temporarily outmanoeuvred the king. The only thing that made this different to previous occasions was that they got a document to prove it.

The Magna Carta went a long way to defining what the early thirteenth-century baronage considered was their duty to the king and also what they considered were the king's obligations to them. It would be pointless to mention many of its provisions here, partly because it was in many ways a pretty ephemeral document and more importantly because it had little to do with royal forests. Three clauses, however, were inserted that had a direct bearing on forest law, two of which – those now quoted – give a fair idea of how much the nobility had come to resent these laws.

> 47. All forest created in our reign shall be immediately disafforested, and similarly river-banks which we have reserved for our sport during our reign shall be again thrown open.
> 48. All oppressive practices relating to forests, warrens and river-banks, and the malpractices of foresters, warreners, the sheriffs and their officers, and river-bank keepers shall, in every county, be the immediate subject of inquiry by twelve sworn knights of the same county, elected by the worthy men of the county; and within forty days of such inquiry, all abuses shall be stamped out, never more to be renewed, by the agency of the said knights; provided always that we, or our justiciar if we are out of England, have been previously informed.

This was a reversal for John – but it is doubtful whether he ever had any intention of carrying out much of his charter, let alone this particular part. Within months he had outmaneouvred the baronage by declaring himself the vassal of the Pope, who promptly declared that he would excommunicate anyone who attempted to impose their will upon his new subject. Excommunication – which removed a man from all benefits of religion in this world and the next was a dire threat and the baronage now hesitated to challenge the king. Yet all were not intimidated. Civil War erupted the following year and, though it was in fact ended by John's death from dysentry, had he lived John would almost certainly have defeated his enemies.

Power was now back with the baronage, for John's successor was his infant son Henry and during his minority the country was to be run by a council drawn from the Church and baronage. In 1217 William Marshall, the regent, was to publish in the name of Henry III, the Charter of the Forest, the seventeen clauses of which embodied the results of the inquiry promised in Clause 48 of John's Charter. It is the Charter of the Forest which was inadvertently responsible for the christening of John's original charter. Because it was smaller than its predecessor the lawyers now termed the earlier one the Magna – and the name has persisted.

In the Charter of the Forest the barons launched an all-out attack on the monarch's rights under forest law. They wiped out the additional rights and extensions of forest land that had come into being during the reigns of John, Richard I and Henry II and re-established forest law as it had been at the end of the reign of hardpressed and wayward Stephen. Meetings of forest courts were restricted to three a year and it was declared that only forest officials need attend them – thus abolishing the powers of the royal forest justices. The power of the foresters was cut back and the provisions for the lawing of dogs was redefined to the point where it was virtually inoperable. The Charter declared that any freeman – ie., anyone of the rank of knight and above – had the right, presuming he did not infringe on that of his neighbours, to make within the forest a mill, fishpond, or drain and to keep hawks, eagles, falcons or herons. He also had the right to pasture cattle on his land within the forest, to allow his pigs to roam the woodlands and to extend his arable land into the areas of the forest within his ownership. Given all this there was now very little for which anyone could be fined within the forests.

The Charter even went so far as to make an inroad into the royal prerogative of the chase when it declared that:

> Any archbishop, bishop, earl or baron who shall pass through our forests shall be allowed to take one or two deer in the presence of

the forester should he happen to be present. If the forester is not there, let the hunter sound his horn lest he be seen to do it by stealth.

It should, however, not be forgotten that on their own lands the barons, both Church and secular, were just as jealous of their own rights of the chase as the king had been of his. Local courts could fine the commoner, in proportion, just as heavily as the king's court had fined the barons – barons, too were often short of money. If the rights of the 'freeman' improved under the Charter of the Forest it was the rights of the aristocracy which improved far more.

The reign of Henry III was a long one – fifty-six years in fact – and much of it was spent by the king in a struggle to win back what the barons had gained from the Crown during his minority. Magna Carta was reissued a number of times with various of its more forceful clauses ommitted and the Charter of the Forest was progressively weakened. The king's forest rights and extensions of forest land continued to be a point of contention with the nobility and were a contributing cause to the civil war known as the Baron's War, which occurred toward the end of Henry's reign. It was this war which led to the calling of what has been termed 'the first English parliament', though its resemblance to a modern parliament can only be said to have lain in the imagination of some later historians. For a time the rebellious baronage were quite successful under the leadership of the Earl of Leicester, Simon de Montfort. But, after the defeat of the two baronial armies at Kenilworth and Evesham in 1265 and the death of de Montfort, his two eldest sons and many of their leading supporters, the King – or rather his son Edward, soon to be Edward I – was once more paramount.

Yet the days of all-mighty royal power in both the forests and the country at large were numbered. Edward I was the last of England's truly omnipotent and ruthless medieval monarchs and the hedonistic activities of his son Edward II were amongst the factors that, in his reign, were to produce yet another civil war, his ultimate assassination with the conivance of his French wife and a royal authority that lay in tatters. Edward II was succeeded by the infant Edward III and for some time the regency was exercised by his mother Queen Isabella and her lover, the ambitious head of the house of Mortimer. Edward I had, however, promised, in 1297, to limit the extent of the royal forest and to reform the forest law and, in 1327, Isabella and Mortimer accepted the limits he had promised as the basis for future forest-law administration.

The later medieval application of forest law was still to give rise to individual outcries and to inflict hardship in some areas. But henceforth it was not to figure as a national grievance amongst the landed aristocracy until Stuart times. England's later medieval kings were now first to be too involved with foreign wars and later with the struggle of the Wars of the Roses to risk alienating support by instance on forest-law rights. The Tudors also were to be more concerned with other matters – mostly with the Church and fears of foreign invasion – to bother with the forests; and by the time James I came to the throne the forest laws had largely lapsed.

But the years of the early Stuarts saw England largely removed from the threat of invasion. This, in turn, liberated an increasingly powerful Parliament from supporting the monarchy at almost any price in the cause of national unity. The possibilities of conflict shifted from the foreign to the domestic front and collision between the king and Parliament was almost an inevitability. In order to raise finance through Parliament the monarchy would have to make political concessions and the Stuart monarchs, far from contemplating the further deplation of royal power, were in favour of strengthening it. In simple terms this meant going to Parliament for money as infrequently as possible and making every effort to raise it by other means.

One means open to the Crown was to attempt to revive the lapsed forest laws and to apply them to areas which had now been long disafforested. James I made some moves in this direction, but it was Charles I who went furthest – in the New Forest he was even to support his revived claim by releasing imported wilf boars. In 1629 Charles did away with his troublesome Parliament and was not to summon it again for eleven years. He now had to find ways of supplying the royal treasury without Parliament's support and he did this partly by resorting to the ancient rights of the royal prerogative. One of these included an attempt to revive the forest law and forest land on a large scale and from 1634 to 1640 large sums were raised by this means. It was said that extensions of the New Forest to its ancient limits would cost the Earl of Southampton £2,000 a year in fines and, for alleged encroachment on Rockingham Forest, the Earl of Salisbury was fined £20,000 and the Earl of Westmoreland £19,000.

Not only did Charles revive forest law in places where forest land had not existed for more than two centuries but he also augmented the royal coffers by the sale of forest land which did exist. This often included the rescinding of common rights in areas of forest land which were sold, as in Malvern Chase where the sale of part of the chase was followed by serious riots at Upton on Severn, the region's 'capital'. In the Forest of Dean a large area was sold to Sir John Wyntour of Lydney – though here common rights do not seem to have been affected – and resulted in the wholesale disafforesting of much of the region. Thus, while in some areas Charles was alienating the landowners in others he was alienating the commoners. But the effect of his forest policy on the landowners was to prove most damaging to his later cause.

Often these men were not the descendants of the traditional aristocracy of feudal times, but the first generation descendants of the 'new men' of the Tudor period. They were an aristocracy of capital rather than an aristocracy of tradition whose flimsy links with the machinery of royal power had been forged not by centuries but by recent circumstance. Very often as Puritan as the Parliamentary extremists they viewed this area of Charles's activities as one more extension of the royal tyranny. To them Charles, with his army of tax-gatherers, was not so much a king as the head of an arbitrary beaurocracy. In the years immediately prior to the Civil War, however, the Forest Laws, as Clarendon was to say in his *History of the Rebellion* "Lighted most upon people of quality and honour, who thought themselves above ordinary oppressions, and therefore like to remember it with more sharpness".

In 1640 Charles was once more forced to summon his Parliament – the Long Parliament – which pressed into action a heady programme of political reform that was to end with the confrontation of the Civil War. Little of the King's action during the years of extra-Parliamentary Government escaped attention and on 7th August 1641 an Act was passed restoring the boundaries of the royal forests to their limitations of 1623. Thus was the Stuart attempt to revive the forest laws undone. The Stuart policy had done nothing for the forests themselves, in fact it had only led to even greater disafforestation. Extensions of forest land had been mere technicalities which had resulted in an increased royal revenue, but in no policy of re-planting. In fact, in those areas of actual forest land which were disafforested on a large scale following their sale there was to be no policy of re-afforestation either. This was to prove a near disaster.

England was no longer the well-wooded country it had been in early medieval times. The needs of farming, of expanding towns and villages, of shipbuilding and of rapidly increasing industry had all cut into the forest lands. The increase in iron-manufacture meant that large areas of the Weald were forest no longer, much of the New Forest had been cleared for agriculture. In the Midlands the forests of Feckenham and Horewell had shrunk greatly and Arden was no longer timbered, while in the North iron-working had practically denuded the Furness peninsula. All over the country the story was the same; woodlands were rapidly shrinking before new and expanding technologies and little was yet being done to replenish the increasing annual loss. Very soon it was not to be the needs of game, nor even the need for revenue that was to be the main preoccupation of government in relation to the surviving areas of forest, but the provision of timber for the needs of the Navy.

The woodlands were not really wild places any more. True, one would still have found difficulty in walking by night through the deeper recesses of Charnwood or the New Forest, but the days of trackless miles of timberland were gone forever. The deer were still plentiful in their preserves, but the wild boar was extinct in the south and midlands, though it lingered in the north as late as 1683 and possibly in the Scottish border even into the early eighteenth century. Wolves, too, had also disappeared in most of England by the mid sixteenth century, and the last recorded wolf in Britain is said to have been killed near Dollgellau in 1785. England was becoming a tame, domestic, increasingly civilized place compared to the realm that had been known it its medieval kings. The surviving forest lands were soon to be looked at with new eyes and were standing at the threshold of the first age of modern conservation.

3

Verderers, Commoners and People

The very concept of 'common land' would seem to date back to times when the idea of the private and individual holding of land was scarcely recognised. Large scale private land-owning probably first appeared on our shores with the coming of the Romans, for it is rather doubtful if the society of the Iron-Age Celts could be classed as one essentially based on private capital. From an economic and legal viewpoint it was the remnants of a Roman capitalist society that was overthrown during the years of the Saxon settlement and in its place was established a society which viewed land as being held in common for the good of all its inhabitants.

Originally almost all land would have been considered as the common property of all, thus, in the tenth century, we find Sherwood Forest – covering an area very much larger than the present woodland – described simply as Scirwuda – the shire wood. This seems to imply that it was a tract of woodland common to all the inhabitants of the shire. Earlier the north-Oxfordshire forest of Wychwood is described as Hwiccewuda – or wood of the Hwicce, the original Anglo-Saxon inhabitants of the kingdom of the Hwicce centred upon Worcester but covering much of Oxfordshire and Gloucestershire as well. This seems another case of a large tract of woodland being held in common by the inhabitants of a very wide area. In the south the forest heathland of Ytene – later the New Forest – bore a title which meant no more than 'of the Jutes', intended, again, to convey that the whole area was held by its inhabitants in common. Of course, there was also the 'waste' – areas in which no common rights or common ownership applied, or rather in which there was no one to apply them. But these three examples serve to illustrate that there were extensive tracts of sparsely settled land in which the Anglo-Saxon commoners had a vested interest from very early times.

The establishment of the principle of private ownership of land was a very gradual process in Anglo-Saxon England. The vill, or group of land-based freemen, practised an agricultural economy divided between arable cultivation of allotments, which seem to have been allocated via a system of annual rotation, and pasturage of pigs, sheep and cattle over land deemed to be held in common for this purpose. Originally all untilled land would have been considered common to all; though well before the Norman invasion, pressure of population was to limit such common land to use by the inhabitants of neighbouring villages.

In time holes began to appear in the fabric of the principle which, to paraphrase Lincoln, declared that all of the land belongs to all of the people all of the time. As England developed into an increasingly centralized state the crown came to possess large holdings of its own and grants of land were also to be the beginnings of manorial organisation which differed from that of the freeman's vill in that here a lord held land, most of which was divided up amongst the various gradations of peasant and whose rental was largely rendered in the form of services provided for the manorial lord on his own demesne.

These, and other developments, often led to a loss of common land but only rarely to a loss of common rights upon that land. Thus, although private landholding came into existence in Anglo-Saxon England it was largely brought about with the retention of certain rights of common useage. This was an economic necessity for the removal of such rights as pannage – the right to pasture swine in woodland – pasturage, turbary – the right to gather turf, peat and bracken – and estovers – the right to gather wood for necessary building repairs – would have led to the collapse of England's peasant economy and undoubtably to local rebellion. In cases where common rights were disregarded such rebellions did sometimes occur.

When the Royal Forests were originally created common

rights were largely respected, both by Cnut and Edward the Confessor. Even William I, despite his new Laws of the Forest, to some extent respected common rights within the forests. In many ways the Crown allowed common rights to continue because they were convenient to both the commoners and the game in that allowing pannage and pasturage within the forests helped to check the spread of undergrowth, just as the right of estovers helped to keep the forests free of dead and fallen timber.

Again, even a legal code as ferocious as the Forest Law could often be manipulated by the forest commoners. Although it was declared that royal game should be free to roam wherever they wished within the forest boundaries, the inhabitants of the forest were also required to fence their holdings to protect the cover against the depredations of their own animals. Thus the royal game did not have a completely free range within the forest and, by the application of common rights, were not the only animals roving there. The deer were to be restricted even further, especially in the New Forest, when it was found that they were destroying new growth in the forest. Coppices of saplings were enclosed by surrounding them with a deep ditch lined with furze. These saplings were needed, not so much to add to the density of the cover, but to provide material for the daub and wattle buildings of the time. In 1236 came Henry III's Statute of Merton – sometimes called the Commons Act – which attempted to preserve common rights on both lands held in common and those which had passed into private ownership. From now on the Law of the Forest compromised, though the Statute of Merton did not prevent the almost continual shrinkage of both common lands and common rights.

Yet, although common land tended to be absorbed and enclosed by individual landowners through the Middle Ages and right up to the middle of the last century with the common rights on such lands of tenure disappearing either at once or over a period of time, this process was not quite so marked in some of the forest regions. Today some of the largest areas over which common rights are exercised in England are the former Royal-Forest regions including the New Forest, the Weald, Epping Forest and the Forest of

Dean. In all but the last mentioned of these, common rights are now well-defined. Other large tracts in which common rights have survived are the non-woodland Royal-Forest areas of Dartmoor and Exmoor. In most of these areas the common rights are now guarded by strong local Commoners Associations. Common rights also exist in various other open spaces, including a large number of village greens and in some of England's upland regions. In the case of the village greens, however, the growth of the commuter villages means that there exist few commoners who exercise agrarian rights and the common usage is more likely to be limited to village cricket.

But much former common land has disappeared. In many cases its loss brought little protest from a peasantry which was already cowed and scarcely aware of what was happening in the enclosure movements of the sixteenth and eighteenth centuries. However, some enclosures did produce sizeable protests. In the reign of Charles I there was considerable disturbance at Upton-on-Severn when the Crown attempted to sell off a large area of Malvern Chase where the local inhabitants had long enjoyed the traditional rights of common. There were serious riots in the town and the sale had to be called off – though it later went through. Serious rioting was also to occur in the early nineteenth century when the Oxfordshire common of Otmoor was enclosed. The inhabitants of seven neighbouring parishes had enjoyed rights of common on the moor for many centuries and these they lost when the moor was enclosed in 1814. Many of the poorer commoners were not even able to afford the cost of enclosing their portion of the moor. The military had to be called out to quell the local disorders and, in 1829, further riots broke out when the judgement of a local court seemed to make the original Enclosure Act illegal. The Oxford Militia and the Yeoman Cavalry were called in, there was a confrontation with the dispossessed commoners and prisoners were taken. These, however, were later to be released by the crowd at Oxford's St Giles' Day Fair – for popular opinion was very much on the side of the Otmoor commoners. When the prisoners were recaptured the sentences were very light partly because the local magistrates to some extent sympathised with the Otmoor men's plight, and partly because it was feared that severe sentences would only provoke further outbreaks of rioting. Otmoor simmered on the edge of revolt for many years afterward and was to be the scene of frequent disturbances for local opinion hardened to the point where it was considered that the government had 'stolen' Otmoor from those who had been entitled to use it. But, in general, the commons and common rights of England died quietly, as did the peasant commoners whose existence had been so dependent upon them.

Certain forest areas, of course, were largely to lose their rights of common as they became gradually disafforested. This was to be the case in respect of such forests as Feckenham, Rockingham and the ancient Forest of Leicester which, like Sherwood, would seem once to have been a shire wood. In general rights of common were mainly extinguished during the eighteenth and nineteenth centuries as the process of enclosure ate up local common land – in many cases the former manorial 'waste' – and left the ability to exercise common rights over what did remain in the hands of a small number of wealthy landowners. It was to a large extent, this that led to the implementation after 1795, of the system of rural dole, known as 'the Speenhamland system'. Men and boys, the descendants of men who, only a few years earlier had been the independent heart of the English countryside, could now, if they were unemployed, be herded into gangs under the control of parish officers and hired out for farm and other work to the highest bidder. This was a form of bondage worse than anything ever inflicted by the Normans and was a major reason for the disposessed peasantry rising against their masters in the ill-fated Agricultural Labourer's Revolt of 1830. The support for this revolt was not very great in most of the remaining forest areas, for here the commoners lacked such a wholesale grievance. But the failure of revolt certainly intensified the 'rural exodus' which was to continue to depopulate the countryside well into the present century.

Looked at from another angle, however, it is difficult to see how the enclosure movement could have failed to fall upon the English countryside. In the late eighteenth century farming, like all other forms of production, was becoming industrialized. Just as former domestic production had been concentrated and enclosed in the unit of the factory so agriculture came also to be enclosed in large units of private ownership. The older means of working were held to be inefficient, especially by such 'new men' as Arthur Young who could not understand why the peasant preferred to work in the time honoured way rather than become a part of what the new theorists considered to be a more economic system. In fact, however, from the point of view of the English peasant, the old system gave far greater rewards than the new. But England was becoming an urban society and subsistence farming was to fall before that which catered for an urban market. It was the growth of England's towns and, more especially the growth of the population of those towns, that indirectly killed off much of the nation's common land and most of its commoners. In an urban, industrialized society rooted in the concept of private ownership, the exercise of common rights at large tend to sound vaguely like political anarchy.

While the nineteenth-century enclosure movement was extinguishing English common rights, the areas of Royal Forest, precisely because they were already in some degree enclosed regions, actually allowed some common rights to persist. The point here is that the royal forest areas had been enclosed though as the same time still allowing for the exercise of traditional rights by commoners living on their fringes. Later enclosures tended to divide common land up amongst the commoners who thus forewent their earlier rights in favour of private ownership. It was precisely because the Crown no longer wished to break up its property that common rights have continued in the forest regions. These rights are now clearly defined in law – which was not the case at the close of the eighteenth century – and are defended with such tenacious zeal that it normally requires an Act of Parliament to remove or alter them.

Legal clarity over most common rights now seems to have been achieved in all the forests – with the exception of the Forest of Dean in which a certain amount of confusion still exists. Here just what constitutes a common right and just who can claim to be a commoner is complicated by historical circumstance. The freeminers are in a class of their own. They appear to have gained the earliest of their rights, that of mining for iron-ore in the forest, as a reward for services rendered as sappers in the Welsh and Continental wars of the thirteenth and fourteenth centuries. But they had probably been exercising such 'rights' for a long time before this and their acceptance by the Plantagenat kings was largely a matter of putting the local record straight. This early right later came to be extended to include the mining of other minerals; including coal, and this too came to assume the states of a common right.

The forest had been a royal forest since at least the reign of Edward the Confessor. At this time the local commoners had paid a fee to the local royal officials in return for the exercise of their 'rights' – which, strictly speaking, were therefore not rights at all. However, the freeminers also came to claim the right of free grazing in the forest as well as the right to use forest timber for their mine workings. Thus there now existed the locally peculiar position of commoners paying for their rights and the freeminers enjoying certain rights for Gratis. The position was even further complicated by the Forest-Law contention that the majority of residents in forest areas were in fact illegal squatters whose rental paid to the Crown was really no more than an annual fine – a quittance – for infringement of Forest Law. Strictly speaking therefore, the freeminers apart, common rights could only be exercised in the Forest of Dean by commoners living outside it and whose livelihood, nevertheless, was largely dependant upon their rights over forest land.

In the reign of Charles I the whole tangled situation was thrown into even greater chaos when the Crown sold a large part of the forest to Sir John Wyntour of Lydney. As an enclosing landlord Wyntour refused to recognise any rights of common – possibly being justified on the ground that what no one else had been able to understand he was hardly to be expected to understand either. He commenced a wholesale felling of timber which was not to be checked until the days of the Commonwealth.

At the Restoration the forest again became the property of the Crown and, in 1668, came the Dean Forest (Reafforestation) Act, which can be called the first modern attempt to introduce some order in the medieval confusion of its administration. The position however, was now further complicated by the growing number of squatters in the forest – something which was to affect many other forest and common land areas. They claimed to be exercising an ancient right whereby if a chimney could be erected and drawing smoke between sunrise and sunset the builder was entitled to build a house at the spot. This picturesque custom, however, was not so much a right as a rumour and went ahead largely because the royal officials, verderers and so on were understandably just as nonplussed about the state of the law regarding the forest as the rest of its inhabitants.

The Act of 1668 did not specifically outlaw squatting but it settled the bounds of the forest, allowed the enclosure of a further 11,000 acres for timber and confirmed common rights as those which had been legally enjoyed in 1634, when Sir John Wyntour had first taken over. This was really not so much an attempt to clarify the medieval situation as to prevent it being further misinterpreted. The Act was primarily framed not to deal with common rights but with the conservation of local timber for the expanding needs of the Navy.

A little earlier, in 1663, some attempt had been made to regulate the activities and status of the freeminers. A freeminer was said to be a man aged twenty-one or over who had been born within the Hundred of St Briavel's – which was roughly equal to the extent of the forest itself – and who had worked at least one year and one day in the Dean mines. Such a man could apply for the grant of a gale – a specific area of land from which to mine. Royalty on any iron-ore so mined would be collected by the king's official known as the Gaveller.

In this year the Court of Mine Law seems to have replaced the former authority of the Gaveller and his officials as the body regulating the operations of the freeminers. It is possible however, that the court had been in existence for some time before, although there are no records of this. The Court was presided over by the Constable of St Briavel's or his deputy and the Gaveller was also present. Cases were heard before a jury of freeminers. Initial pleas were heard by a jury of twelve and appeals went first to a jury of twenty-four and if pressed again, to a jury of forty-eight beyond which there was no further appeal. There were no lawyers present at these hearings and only the parties to the actual disputes could plead. The Court also fixed prices for minerals and set output targets as well as running the forerunner of a modern scheme of industrial compensation. The Court seems to have enjoyed a fitful existence in its early years but ceased to function after 1754.

The late seventeenth century also saw the Verderers' Court move from its old home at St Briavel's Castle to the Speech House – now a well-known hotel. It was this court which was charged with limiting the number of illegal dwellings being erected in the forest, besides being responsible for the new policy of replanting, the general conservation of timber and the operation of rights of common.

Much of the forest timber was to be taken for naval needs during the Napoleonic wars and, in 1808, the Dean Forest Timber Act authorized extensive replanting besides re-enacting most of the provisions of the Act of 1668. Other Acts were to inaugurate different planting policies and in 1855 the royal deer – for whom the area had once been maintained – officially disappeared, though animals still take preference to vehicles on the forest roads.

During the nineteenth century the iron-ore mining industry went into a decline largely due to competition from the North and South Wales, though the last mine, was not to close until 1939. Coal mining however, increased greatly until, by 1900, the Dean coalfield was producing in the region of a million tons *per annum*. But this, too, was to fall away, especially after the First World War, though some freeminers still remain to work a number of small pits selling their coal to the National Coal Board. These small pits are now the only ones in private ownership in England.

In 1924 the Forestry Commission took over the running of the Forest with a co-ordinating committee consisting of representatives of the Commission, the local authorities and the Verderers. In 1938 the region was declared a National Forest Park, the first of its kind in the country. Legally this now added more confusion to the existing situation by providing certain rights of public access to some areas of the forest.

In 1959 some attempt was made to reconcile the conflicting laws relating to common and other rights in the forest. Again the Act of 1668 was taken as the basic point of reference and it was now declared that whatever common rights there were in the forest could only be exercised as they had been at the time of Wyntour's 1634 take-over. Establishing just what rights had been exercised in 1634 and by whom was to prove a rather laborious task. In many instances it was to prove completely inconclusive. Moreover no resident within the bounds of the Forest was held to be able to claim the exercise of common rights as it was illegal for anyone to reside within a royal forest. Rights which had been acquired after 1634 were declared not to be common rights at all and to have no basis in law. Thus, although many thousands of sheep roam the forest at will, they do not appear to do so by common right as sheep were not introduced into the forest until the late seventeenth century. It would seem that they are there on sufferance from the Crown.

From a technical viewpoint there would appear to be now no common rights within the actual bounds of the Royal Forest, though there would appear to be common rights on those stretches of neighbouring forest land such as Tiddenham Chase and Bearse Common. There are still freeminers, legal common rights in the purlieus of the forest and illegal 'rights' being exercised within the forest. The public has a limited right of access and in general the legal situation in the area is still very confused, notwithstanding the various edicts of the Forestry Commission, local authorities, the Court of Verderers and now the Department of the Environment.

The majority of England's other forest areas do not have to labour under the disadvantage of such a legal tangle. The modern history of the New Forest can be said to date from the Deer Removal Act of 1851 which, while it did not exactly remove the deer made them secondary to the conservation of timber. There has been a steady decline in their numbers. In 1851 more than 8,000 deer were recorded roaming in the New Forest whilst, almost a century later in 1945, this figure had dropped to 4,582. The Act of 1851 authorized the enclosure of a further 10,000 acres for timber and was prepared to recognise the commoners and common rights in the area as long as it could be shown that such rights had been continually exercised since 1800. Compared to the situation that was to arise in the Forest of Dean this was a very liberal provision.

In 1877 the New Forest Act reconstituted the ancient Court of Verderers, who from now on were to function primarily to protect the rights of the commoners. The Act also limited the powers of the Crown to enclose land and required that any further enclosure must have the specific assent of Parliament. In 1923 the Forestry Commission took over the New Forest from the Crown working in conjunction with the Court of Verderers. Prior to a revision of the existing situation it was found that common rights were exercised in just short of 45,000 instances – this survey being made in 1947. Under the New Forest Act of 1949 the Court of Verderers was reconstituted and the Nature Conservancy made its first appearance on the local scene. The area of the New Forest was now stated to be 92,365 acres, roughly two-thirds of this being in Crown ownership. To this figure could be added some 6,000 acres of nearby common lands.

Over the New Forest as a whole common rights are extensively used, not only the usual right of pasturage, but the nowadays far less usual rights of pannage and estovers. In fact, of all the woodland forest regions – to differentiate them from such areas as Dartmoor and Exmoor – the New Forest is the one in which common rights are still most widely used. With local administration here firmly on the side of the commoners there seems very little likelihood that their rights will be diminished in the foreseeable future.

Perhaps at this juncture urban dwellers should be cautioned not to expect New Forest commoners – or those of any other forest region come to that – to be picture-book peasants of the smock, gaiters- and straw-sucking variety. If the idea of a simple-minded English peasantry was ever based in much more than myth – which is to be doubted – then it has by now not the slightest foundation in fact. If we do still possess a simple-minded peasantry it is much more likely to be found engaged in such mechanistic occupations as the operation of the machines which mould babies' plastic rattles than in coping with the many technical tasks that go to make up the modern agrarian economy. This is not to say that the commoners do not produce the occasional rogue layabout. In most cases however, this is no more than the affluent and ostentatious breed who perhaps doubles as a young executive living in chintz splendour in his desecrated, much extended forest cottage. In their contribution to the whole such irrelevancies add little more than local colour.

If the commoners of the New Forest can be numbered in their thousands then those of Epping and Hainault Forests – the surviving remnants of the once vast Forest of Waltham – are little more than a handful. Epping is a most peculiarly shaped woodland, a wedge of forest land extending from the outer limits of London into the beginnings of rural Essex, being twelve miles in length but at no time more than two miles in width. Like most English forests from the Middle Ages onward, Epping shrank continually and, up to the middle of the last century, the forest was in great danger of disappearing completely as enclosures snipped steadily away at its boundaries. Local commoners had little hope of redress as the Court of Verderers had long since lapsed. The situation, however, was saved by the Corporation of London which, as the owners of Ilford Cemetery bordering on Wanstead Flats, held important rights of common in the forest. Other commoners invoked the support of the Corporation who were instrumental in re-establishing the Court of the Verderers. This successfully pressed for the re-opening of illegal enclosures in the forest and was instrumental in preventing new ones.

This was merely a holding operation. In 1878 the Epping Forest Act was passed which appointed the Corporation as Conservators of Epping Forest. The forest ceased to be held by the Crown which maintained only the power to make a titular appointment to the office of Ranger. The forest was declared to be an open space for use by the public for recreation, though the rights of the commoners were recognised. Enclosure was to be limited to that necessary for such things as replanting. The Corporation became the sole owner of land within the forest. Keepers were appointed to patrol it and these are now uniformed, having the power of special constables and with regular 'beats' within the area. There are also other keepers whose activities cover less defined areas as well as part-time reeves who represent the verderers and the commoners. A small herd of deer is maintained, though their numbers are a mere fraction of those to be found in the New Forest.

As the outer limits of London have expanded during the present century agricultural land around the edge of Epping has rapidly been eaten up so that now only its northern fringe abuts onto what would be termed genuine countryside. This development has meant a steady dwindling in the number of commoners who are able, or wish to avail themselves of common rights. Those few who do, now have considerable powers in the Court of Verderers and have almost the right of veto over any proposed legislation. Complaints have been made that the cattle of those few commoners who still use the forest constitute a nuisance. On the other hand however, many visitors appear to welcome their presence as adding to the rurality of the surroundings. Personally I feel it would be a pity if the cattle were removed for Epping would then cease to be a forest and become, in fact if not in name, just another London park.

The Forests of Dean, Epping and the New Forest are large areas where common rights can be said to exist under some recognisable framework. In the case of many other forest-regions the position is, unfortunately, far less clear and when attempts are made to achieve administrative clarity these often seem to lead to a further shrinkage of common rights. Cannock Chase for example, covers an area of 16,000 acres, but of this only 1,000 acres in the parish of Colwick can be said to have rights of common. Much of the remainder of the Chase – which is a coalfield as well as a Forestry-Commision plantation – is, however, open to the public under the terms of the 1949 National Parks Act.

In the Weald there exist no common rights in St Leonard's Forest. However, under various Ashdown-Forest Acts, common rights are exercised on the Ashdown-Forest land of which Earl de la Warr is lord of the manor. These are exercised by in the region of one thousand commoners.

As one would expect little common land now exists in the disafforested areas such as Rockingham Forest and Malvern

Chase. In the Forest of Arden there is very little common land, except in the area of Earlswood. In the Feckenham-Forest district the most notable survivals are the 168 acres of Kempsey Common and other commons in this parish bring the total of common land here up to 253 acres. Common land of 132 acres survives at Pershore.

In Shropshire's Clun Forest common rights have largely disappeared except at Black Hill and Newcastle Fron. There appear to be no surviving common rights in Wychwood, Savernake, Charnwood or Sherwood Forests, the latter appearing to have lost its rights when much of the area was enclosed in the period when it became better known as the Dukeries. In the Delamere Forest region some rights do survive. Most notably these are rights on Knutsford Heath which is jointly administered by the Nether Knutsford Freeholders and the lord of the manor. The rights include those of pasturage and the digging of clay.

In certain areas – not necessarily forests – common rights are protected by organisations such as The New Forest Commoners' Defence Association, the Cornwall Commoners' Association and the picturesquely titled Hatherleigh Potboilers who control the rights on Exmoor's Hatherleigh Moor. In many places where they do remain, common rights are now being zealously guarded. But it would seem that those exercised in some areas only by the occasional farmer are bound to fall by the wayside. In general what common rights that ultimately survive will probably be those exercised over relatively wide areas where the commoners' own associations and local legal institutions will ensure their continuance.

Common rights are a very different matter to public access. In many instances the two concepts are in conflict. In earlier times, of course, when all Englishmen would have been commoners of one sort or another there could have been no such clash of interests. However, we live in the twentieth century and not in Anglo-Saxon England. But most of what common land does remain is now common only to a few locally based commoners. The vast majority of English people possess no common rights on English soil. Apart from the surviving commoners the only person with rights of common over common land is the lord of the manor. The lord of the manor has the additional right of being able to shoot game on the common and may have some other rights, such those relating to minerals. In many cases lords of the manor are now corporate bodies such as local authorities or government organisations such as the National Coal Board. Strictly speaking the House of Commons – or more correctly the House of Commoners – has long been a misnomer. It would be more correct to rename it after its American counterpart, the House of Representatives.

The general public has some rights of access to common land under the Law of Property Act of 1925. This gave the public right of access to commons in London and other urban areas for air and recreation. In some rural areas local lords of the manor have given various rights of access to common land in their ownership. As is the case with the urban commons, however, this generally includes certain restrictions regarding motor vehicles. Except in cases where a public highway crosses common land motor vehicles can generally only be driven over it in connection with common rights, such as rounding up sheep or cattle pastured on the common.

In the countryside at large the public has rights of access via public footpaths and bridleways. Given our urbanized society some of these rights sound distinctly bucolic. On a recognised footpath the "public has a right of way on foot only" but on a bridleway the public has a right of passage on foot, on horseback or leading a horse and may occasionally also have the right to drive animals on the hoof. The Countryside Act of 1968 extended the public rights on a bridleway to include pedal cyclists, but stipulated that cyclists must give way to pedestrians and riders on horseback. It may also be illegal to use a perambulator or push-chair on a public footpath – which is not a pavement – or bridleway, though no decision has ever been taken on this.

Although many footpaths are now well signposted some are still so badly defined that the casual walker may often find himself in the unintentional position of a trespasser. Public footpaths in the English countryside are still vanishing at an alarming rate. While a few may be said to have outlived their purpose, the efforts of such organizations as the Ramblers' Association to preserve many more for public use deserve all the support they can get, especially in a time when there is so much pressure on those open spaces still left to us.

It may be worth while stating that it is illegal for a landowner to obstruct a public footpath, even by so much as the erection of a stile. The old and often stated tradition of a right of closure of a public path if it has not been known to have been used for a year and a day has no legal basis. A footpath may only be closed with the consent of the appropriate local authority which has to be satisfied "that the path is not needed for public use". The closure must be confirmed by the Secretary of State for the Environment who must be satisfied that the path is rarely used by the public and that its closure will not have an adverse effect on any land served by it.

In many forest areas – and in other parts of the countryside as well – the walker will occasionally find himself faced by notices declaring that "Trespassers will be prosecuted". Quite often this sort of notice will only be found after one has been inadvertently trespassing on land for some while. However, trespass is a crime only if it can be said to have caused damage or to have aggravated the owner of the land. In the case of the latter it is not casual but repeated trespass that must be alleged. It could be said that the casual trespasser caused damage the moment he broke a blade of grass. But landowners who take civil proceedings against the casual trespasser – who may only have picnicked on land he thought was common – can in general expect little sympathy from the courts and may find that they have to bear the costs of the case themselves.

The courts will, however, take a more serious view if the trespasser has caused damage to such things as crops, fences or has let cattle stray. In such cases the owner is entitled to claim compensation. The law will also take a dim view of illegal shooting – for only the owner of land is entitled to shoot over it unless he has given specific permission to others to do so. Fishing rights are also strongly protected and unlicensed fishing can result in a civil action for trespass or a criminal action under the 1968 Theft Act. However, the law places the onus for the protection from injury of children on private land on the owner. If a landowner is aware that children are in the habit of entering his land because it has an interesting pond, a deserted barn or some other attraction it is his duty to see that it is rendered reasonably safe. Children who are invited onto private land by the owner or his employees are naturally considered to be in the owner's responsibility.

All this would seem to imply that Mr and Mrs General Public have very few rights in the English countryside. In general this is true. However, there are a number of exceptions. In the years since 1945 the public has, through various Acts of Parliament, gained the right of access for recreation and exercise to a number of areas of land. Certain areas controlled by the Forestry Commission are now open to the public and the Commission is empowered to create bye-laws for the preservation and protection of timber and the general amenities of the area. However, these bye-laws must not interfere with common rights and in the Forest of Dean and the New Forest must also have the assent of the Verderers. The Commission is empowered to provide facilities for visitors on land managed by it including camping-sites, footpaths, nature trails, places for refreshment, accommodation and information, car parks and so on.

The general public also has right of access to the National Parks, such as the Peak District – though the administering body can limit this. On a small scale there also exists a right of access to country parks created by local authorities under the 1968 Countryside Act. Sites for country parks, which are generally near to towns, can be acquired by compulsory purchase order. Many now include provision for camping and picnic sites and a number have their own nature trails.

Other areas to which the public has a right of access include land over which the local authorities have acquired an access agreement. These apply to such areas as the long-distance footpaths covering Offa's Dyke and the Pennine Way. The public also has a right of access to some land in the ownership of the National Trust where the land was originally given to the Trust for this specific purpose. The Trust is not a government body and land it administers is not exempt from compulsory purchase. The Nature Conservancy however, is a government body. This has powers in respect of a large number of small woodland and other sites. Public access to these is generally limited, though there may exist nature trails and some parts of the reserves may be open to the public at special times. Other government bodies, such as the Central Electricity Generating Board, may also permit limited public access to nature trails and so forth on their land.

At present it is the declared policy of the Forestry Commission to provide greater public access to the areas under its administration. Camping-sites in forest areas have proved to be extremely popular, especially in the New Forest, the Forest of Dean and at Keilder in the Border Forest Park. In Dean the main site is at Christchurch with an overflow site for boy scouts and other youth groups at the riverside. Other smaller areas, such as the Forest of Wyre on the Worcestershire-Shropshire border, also have limited site facilities. The Commission maintains, with some justification, that it is lack of money that has largely prevented the development of further sites and the extension of the overworked facilities of existing ones. Understandably, the picture does not brighten when one comes to the many areas of private woodland being managed along commercial lines. Here access is still, in general, severely limited. However, woodland seems an attraction in itself these days and perhaps some of these may yet relax their present restrictions.

But at the moment, there is considerably more right of public access to the larger English forests than there is to most other areas of the English countryside. The position in modern times, however is far different from that in the old days of Crown control. The Verderers are now no longer primarily Crown officials, but exist largely to protect the rights of the commoners. The surviving forest commoners still exercise their ancient rights which must be respected equally by the public using the forests for recreation, the Forestry Commission using them for industrial purposes and the various local authorities.

In general English people are commoners no longer. Yet they enjoy rights of access to most areas of the major forests. In general these rights have been won and confirmed only in recent years, though there are some exceptions to this as with Epping Forest. The future may well see rights of public access granted over a much wider area of the countryside. Yet it has to be remembered that forestry, like agriculture, is a modern industry and rights of public access must always be weighed against economic considerations. Having won back what rights we have it is only sensible that we see they are exercised with care.

4

Forest Industry

Almost as soon as primitive man emerged from his cave he would have needed a few trees to build a home and perhaps to erect a defensive stockade. Organized industry however, related to the forests can hardly be said to have begun until men began tentatively to exploit the earth's mineral resources. But once men began to work metal – no matter on how small a scale – the forests were in business as industrial centres, for they provided the only known fuel supply.

The Celtic smith of pre-Roman times was an object of near religious veneration. It was he who fused fire and metal not only into objects of usefulness in the forms of harness, cooking vessels and weapons but also into forms of great beauty in the ornaments and jewellery that continued to be made both during and after the Roman occupation in the Celtic areas of Britain. Legends such as those of the Alcester smiths in the Midlands and of Weland the Smith in the south were to survive through the Anglo-Saxon period in England and helped to give the occupation of the smith an element of mystery as well as of technical skill. In the popular imagination the smith had long had something more than a casual connection with Thor and the gods of the old religions.

In Anglo-Saxon times and for most of the medieval period, the mining of most minerals took place in forest regions because here was the most obvious source of fuel. However, for many centuries the existence of mining and metal industries in the forests was not to imply a great wastage of woodland. At this time industry was a rather small-scale affair. Mining especially was limited because of a general absence of pumping machinery, and even where pumping machinery was used it had only a very limited application. It was the danger of flooding that kept medieval mines shallow. Largely because of this there developed, in the major mining regions such as the Weald, the itinerant forge operated by a small group of workers. These not only ran the forge but also mined the ore and felled the trees to convert into charcoal. When the ore ran out or flooding made it impossible to mine further the forge and its workers simply moved on to another part of the forest.

This was the general method of working and in such circumstances the amount of actual metal produced was small and, for the most part, intended for local needs. As society became more complex, however, there began to be a demand for metal working on a national scale. This came especially from the Crown in relation to the munitions for medieval warfare. Although most mining and smelting remained to fulfill purely local needs two centres were to emerge to cater for more than a local trade. These were to be the Forest of Dean and the Weald.

The Forest of Dean was to develop its mining and smelting to the point where it came to be the centre of the medieval English armaments trade. The first large royal order seems to have come from King John, who ordered 2,000 cross-bow bolts for his campaign in Normandy. The work was probably undertaken by a large number of small forges and supplied to the Crown via the forest's resident royal official, the Constable of St Briavel's. Armament manufacture became a basic part of the local economy and arms were not only supplied to the English kings but to the Continent and Scotland as well. It is quite likely that some of the arms used by the Scots to defeat the English at Bannockburn were in fact manufactured by the English themselves in the Forest of Dean. When the first bombards – the precursors of the later cannon – made their appearance it was natural that they too should come to be made in the forest. The bombard was, in fact, not an all-metal gun but a mixture of wood and iron. Because no method had yet been discovered of boring iron, the barrel of the bombard was made of interlocking timbers bound around with iron bands. At first these new weapons – which fired wooden 'cannon balls' and stones as well as heavy shot – were just as likely to kill the bombardiers as the enemy they were firing at. Even Henry V's "great goone, the Kyngesdoughter" which was built under the personal supervision of the warrior king himself, was to explode when firing its first round at the siege of Harlech.

As the Dean iron-industry grew it was largely dominated by two groups of ironmasters – although the small forges operated by a few independent men certainly did not die out. One of these local groups was the Malemort family who operated a number of forges around St Briavel's and came eventually to dominate the local industry. The other was composed of the monks of Flaxley Abbey who engaged in both mining and smelting over a wide area of the forest. Like the monks of Cartmel Abbey in the Furness peninsula and those of Hales Abbey in the West Midlands a large part of their revenue was to be derived from the mining and metal working industries.

It is during this period that it is generally supposed that the Dean freeminers came into existence, although there exists no documentary evidence to support the claim. In the seventeenth century however, officials accepted the general assertion that the freeminers had won their original rights in the forest as a reward for acting as sappers in the medieval wars of the English kings. As medieval warfare – before the development of the cannon – was very often little more than a long series of siege campaigns, sappers were, however invisible, front line troops. Many undoubtedly came from the Forest mines and their reward was doubtless justified.

In later times the rights of the miners were extended from iron-ore mining to include lead and coal – though coal was very little mined during most of the Middle Ages. These rights, while not resting upon a royal award, were nevertheless also officially recognised in the seventeenth century. Just who could and can legally claim to be a freeminer has been discussed in an earlier chapter. Some still exist.

A similar method of working small pits – originally almost surface workings – seems to have been practised by the miners of Worcestershire's Abberley Hills. By the time of Elizabeth I some of these mines had come into the hands of Worcester Corporation and it does not seem that there arose any freemining system here. Quite a number probably served as sappers, just as did those of Dean, in England's medieval wars. It was perhaps their misfortune that their mines did not lie in the midst of a Royal Forest.

The shallow workings of the Dean miners have given rise to at least one peculiarity in the vegetation of the modern forest. In medieval times the miners strengthened the galleries of their mines by driving in pegs made of yew. Being quite near to the surface some of these took root and the clumps of yew to be found in some parts are said to have sprung from these early pit-props.

The needs of the 'bloomeries', as the early forges were called, made great demands on the local timber and the Crown found itself responsible both for the partial destruction of the forest and also for its maintenance. The bloomeries were not the forges where the iron was shaped – these were known as the chafferys – but where the impurities were removed from the iron by continued hammering and reheating. The bars of 'pig iron' were received by them from the furnaces which stood at the beginning of the productive chain. It was in the bloomery that the iron was well and truly wrought.

By various Acts some attempt was made to limit the extent of disafforestation caused by the smelting industry. In general however, such efforts met with little success. By the beginning of the seventeenth century large areas of the forest, especially in the region of Cinderford and around St Briavel's itself, were virtually stripped of woodland. The coexistent Forest of Corse, which ran north-eastward of the main forest, had ceased to exist in all but name.

To some extent the same was true of many other forest areas, such as Cannock Chase – whose charcoal went to fuel the growing iron-working industry of south Staffordshire, of Derbyshire and also of the Weald. As early as the sixteenth century some Wealden furnaces were being let relatively cheaply due to the fact that their local timber supply could not be expected to outlast the term of the lease. Some forges were by now, using an immense quantity of timber. In Sussex the forges of Sheffield and Worth were annually consuming over 10,000 cords of timber – a cord being equal to 125 cubic feet. A beech tree one foot square at 'the stubbe' was estimated to provide one and a half loads of charcoal – and at Tintern's Monkswood Ironworks it was estimated that one year's production would entail the use of at least six hundred such trees. The demand was paralleled in almost all the forest regions and predicted a frightful spate of destruction. It was becoming obvious that the industry – but especially the iron the metal industries – would soon consume England's remaining woodland.

In the latter Middle Ages what could have been the imminent destruction of the Forest of Dean was averted by the growing smelting and charcoal industries tending to move to the Weald which now found its own problem of shrinking timber resources intensified. But the Wealden centre was moving away from the use of local ore in favour of the cheaper iron which was being imported from Spain. However, an influx of refugee Hugenot workers acted as an additional spur to the local industry. One of these, Peter Baude, working in conjunction with Ralph Hogge, a local ironmaster from Buxted, discovered a method of casting cannon in one piece and then of boring them by a process very similar to that used in the boring of bronze cannon. This discovery was to put the Wealden industry far ahead of its rival in the Forest of Dean. It now became the major centre of the industry, a position it was to retain until the mid eighteenth century.

The process of denudation marched steadily on – and not only in the Weald and the Forest of Dean. The ironworks of the Furness Peninsula had been sufficiently known in the fourteenth century for them to merit a number of raids by the marauding Scots, who carried off not only worked iron but the water-powered bellows and other implements of production as well. The Furness peninsula had originally been extensively wooded, but by the mid seventeenth century, most had been denuded of timber by the charcoal burners and even scrubland on the edge of the moors was being pressed into service. Such forests as that of Wyre were being affected not only by nearby industry but also by the demands of the Dean ironworks – and many a Severn barge took its load of charcoal downstream for the iron trade.

The iron and charcoal industries may have been the major drain on the natural resources of England's forests – but they were far from being the only ones. At Nantwich and Droitwich it was the demands of the salt trade which ate with increasing appetites into Delamere and Feckenham forests. In the case of Delamere some of it was destined to survive. Feckenham however, was to disappear almost completely. Salt had been extracted from brine at Driotwich since long before the arrival of the Romans and when the Romans did find their way into the Midland shires they took over and expanded the industry of 'Salinae'. Salt, in days when there was no other means of preserving food, was something that could not be done without and the settlement, which was almost exclusively involved with salt manufacture, has some claim to be considered the first industrial town in England. At the end of the Anglo-Saxon period there were three hundred salt-houses, each with their vats and furnaces, occupying land in or around Droitwich. The town supplied manors as far south as Buckinghamshire and, despite the wells occasionally drying up, expanded its production throughout the Middle Ages. The forest retreated before the ever increasing demands of the furnaces and by the beginning of the eighteenth century had very largely ceased to exist.

Local industries also cut into the native woodland. Tanneries were prolific users of fuel, so were breweries and even more so brick, tile and glass-making. It was the bringing in of the hop and the establishment of a brewing industry at Alton in Hampshire that was responsible for series inroads into what is now the well-maintained and protected Alice Holt Forest. Glass-making, expanded by refugee Hugenots at Stourbridge in the late sixteenth century bit heavily into Cannock Chase and the Forest of Kinver. Boat building, too, at almost all the riverside towns, was dependent for its raw material on local timber as of course, was most domestic building.

But if it was pre-coal industry's needs for a continual supply of fuel that seriously depleted the major forests it was the growing needs of the Royal Navy for its 'wooden walls' in the seventeenth and eighteenth centuries which threatened to finish off the job. By the end of the period some efforts were being made to enforce the re-planting of some forest areas. But the good intentions of Parliaments were not always carried out and, despite a good many laudable Acts, it was not until the mid nineteenth century that a systematic policy of replanting came to be generally applied.

Most seriously affected by the needs of the Navy was the New Forest. This was one of the few forest areas which was not on ground well-endowed with minerals. In consequence it had, with the exception of its southern shoreline, been largely by-passed by the fury of industry's associated charcoal burners. New-Forest soil, in many parts, was poor and its native oaks did not generally grow tall and straight but, rather were gnarled and somewhat grotesque. Such timbers however, were ideal for use as the 'knees' and 'elbows' of the men-of-war, endowed with a contorted strength that could be well expected to brace the outer timbers of the ships against most things that the raging seas might offer.

The centre of the New-Forest shipbuilding industry was to be found at the now picturesque village of Bucklers' Hard situated at the mouth of the Beaulieu River. It was, however, not the only place where shipbuilding was carried on and both Lymington and Beaulieu itself took part in the industry. The second Duke of Montague had ambitious plans, in the eighteenth century, to turn Bucklers' Hard into a thriving port and town to handle trade from his plantations on the West-Indian island of Lucia. It was the duke who was responsible for the two ranges of red brick cottages which now make the heart of the village, the north row ending in the Master Builder's House, a small, but fine eighteenth-century house with a pedimented doorway. The two rows are separated by a long stretch of green and are stepped down the slight slope that leads to the riverbank. Beyond, on the furthest bank, are the oaks of the Exbury woodlands, fine reminders that this is the edge of forest country. The duke's ambitious plans were destined to be dashed and neither port nor town materialized. The two rows of cottages were the only things to be built and perhaps it was just as well that no 'new town' grew up at this shoreline fringe of the forest.

But if the port and town did not appear, the local shipbuilding industry seems to have managed very well without them. Bucklers' Hard, situated on a deep-water estuary and with the oakwoods of the forest so near at hand, enjoyed an ideal location. The industry was thriving here as early as the sixteenth century, but it was in the eighteenth that it was to enjoy its real hey-day when many of the wooden-walled ships-of-the-line were built here. The most famous of these was undoubtedly the *Agamemnon* which was launched in 1781. It was destined to be commanded by Nelson and to see service in the battles of both Copenhagen and Trafalgar. In its old age it was to be used as cable-layer. Throughout the Napoleonic Wars the local shipbuilding yards were of great importance and 1800 saw the launching of the *Spenser*, a vessel of 1,917 tons with a compliment of over six hundred men.

In the general depression following the end of the Wars however, Bucklers' Hard fell into deepening decline and was to be bypassed by the age of steam which revolutionized shipbuilding as well as much else. A few fishing vessels were built here in the latter part of the nineteenth century but, eventually the old trade ceased completely. But Buckler's Hard is still firmly wedded to the sea. It is now a thriving centre of the leisure sailing type and yachts of all kinds are moored here.

The shipbuilding industry of the eighteenth century did for many parts of the New Forest what the charcoal burners had already done for most of England's other forest regions. The demand for timber during the Napoleonic Wars greatly depleted the local timber supply – and that of the Forest of Dean. It was the great drain on local timber that led, in 1807, to the first real steps being taken to preserve what still remained of the forest and to replant systematically areas which had been deforested.

Little now remains of the ships which once quite literally grew in the forests. There is, of course, Portsmouth's *Victory* – though just how much of this is now original timber it would be difficult to say. There is also, on a somewhat less exhalted plane, the *Cutty Sark* and a few wooden commercial vessels which are now mostly used as training ships. But the great wooden fleets of yesteryear have almost completely rotted into oblivion.

Such has not so uniformly been the case with timber that was used for domestic building. Forest – and former forest – regions are, almost without exception, marked by the presence of half-timbered buildings. Away from the forest, which in past times usually meant in upland or marshy areas, we find domestic buildings largely constructed of local stone as in the

Cotswolds, Dartmoor and the Lake District while in the Fenlands houses were formerly built of rushes and peat-hags. In medieval times domestic building tended to be almost exclusively of local materials (although there were exceptions) and in the forest it was only natural that local people should turn to timber.

As has been already mentioned England was so extensively wooded in Anglo-Saxon times that almost all buildings – including the original Westminster Abbey – were of timber construction. This being so, a continual combination of fire and damp has left us virtually without any architectural remains from those days.

In medieval times it was the exercise of the common rights of house bote and hay bote that accounted for much of the domestic building drain on local timber. House bote allowed the commoner to take wood for the repair and improvement of his house and haybote to take wood for the same purpose for his other buildings, byres, store-sheds and so on. The massive timbers for the cruck-frame constructions of medieval times were taken from the forests and very often these and the massive oak beams of many houses and cottages are all that now survive of the former woodlands. Despite the ecclesiastical longing for permanance in stone, many local churches were also of timber-framed construction as, very largely, were the roofs of many more important ecclesiastical buildings. Apart from buildings many other things were also constructed of timber, including bridges which had a habit of being swept away every so often, and almost all the implements of husbandry including ploughs, carts and even the lowly spade.

Even more than the charcoal burners and the metal trades it was agriculture in and around the forest regions that was most responsible for the continual shrinkage of forest land. Where the charcoal burners had destroyed whole areas of forest there was sometimes at least the possibility – which was occasionally realized – that the area would one day be reafforested. When agriculture moved in to fell the trees and create a completely different pattern of life such a possibility hardly existed. True, under the Laws of the Forest, land which had been appropriated to agricultural use was sometimes restored as forest. But this was usually a mere technicality. It did not necessarily mean the replating of the deafforested area, only that the cleared land was to be unenclosed so that the forest game could again roam freely over it. Once lost to agriculture, forest land was generally lost completely.

The many black and white half-timbered buildings of the Midland shires, especially perhaps, those of the Forest of Arden, Worcestershire and Cheshire are eloquent evidence that these were once well-wooded areas. It was by the continual expansion of domestic building, of agriculture and small scale domestic industry that the forests were gradually attacked from without and by the activities of the charcoal burners and woodcutters in relation to the needs of a more generalized industry that they were attacked from within. Given the needs of an expanding population, plus the maladministration of the royal forest officials themselves, the forests could not have hoped to survive.

Although it was not exactly the case an Act of Parliament of 1503, when contrasting in its preamble the then existing woodland of England with that which had existed in earlier times declared quite simple that the forests had been "utterly destroyed". It was quite true that by then England's formerly vast and near continuous forest cover had largely disappeared. In the following century the diarist Evelyn was to deplore the fact that "truly the waste and destruction of our woods has been so universal that I can conceive of nothing else than universal plantation of all sorts of trees will supply and counter the deficit". By now Evelyn was voicing an opinion that was becoming increasingly felt in government circles. But the well wooded country was a thing of the past and could never hope to be restored. England was the least wooded country in Europe and remains so to this day.

The vast destruction of English woodlands throughout the Middle Ages for the needs of industry argues the existence of an industrial revolution that far predated that which came into being at eighteenth-century Coalbrookdale. There was a rising tide of industrial invention throughout the Middle Ages which lacks definition only because we often do not know the names of the individual innovators nor the precise dates at which their inventions came into use. Industrially, England was far from being a static society. It has long been known that the masons who worked on many of our cathedrals journeyed around the countryside from job to job learning new techniques at one site and then introducing them at another. In fact, this travelling was part of learning the craft of many medieval trades and few men made the grade of master without first having been a journeyman.

This journeying principle, at least to some degree, was very probably true of those engaged in most of the metal trades which, as we have already seen, had their roots in what had originally been an itinerant industry. The metal industries were not so much dependent on the existence of iron-ore as on the existence of wood for fuel. These were times when transportation routes were poor and the metal industries could only succeed where mineral resources and timber supplies were found in combination. Despite the fact that they formed England's third largest industry – after agriculture and the cloth industry – the individual ironworks were small and England's woodlands may conceivably not have suffered so greatly if there had been any conscious policy of replanting. But there was not. Charcoal burners and woodsmen felled the trees in one area and then moved onto another. Natural replacement was far too slow a process ever to keep pace with the demands of industry. In the circumstances, disafforestation on a wide scale was inevitable.

Some attempts were made to control the number of forges working in such areas as the Weald and the Forest of Dean. But royal authority virtually disappeared in the forest for a large part of the fifteenth century when the old aristocracy was busy rending itself to pieces in the family feud that we know as the Wars of the Roses. It was in this period that the iron industry surged forward in a great phase of expansion. The forests were now looked upon largely as cash reserves, rather than game preserves. Financially embarrassed nobles and the rival kings – Edward IV and Henry VI – sold off forest land to keep the war banners flying. It was largely this state of affairs that accelerated the final assault on the forests to the point where the Tudors came to rule over a land where virgin woodland had almost ceased to exist.

Timber was now to be increasingly imported from abroad and industry of almost every kind was faced with a serious fuel crisis. Coal and peat were to be used in some areas – but the iron-smelting industry was one where the use of coal was still impractical because of the impurities its use introduced into the metal – though it was to be discovered that coal could be used for some other iron-working processes.

In the early seventeenth century Dud Dudley, an illegitimate son of the Earl of Dudley, working at Rugeley in South Staffordshire, claimed to have discovered a successful method of smelting iron-ore with coal. Fearing that his success would drive them out of business his local competitors organized gangs of workmen to smash up his furnaces. This was done with such regularity that Dudley seems to have abandoned his efforts. Sir John Wyntour, a little later in the century, was also to claim that he had been able to make use of a similar method and is thought to have used it in the Forest of Dean. But the process remained a closely guarded secret and it was to be another century before England's industry was to be generally liberated from its dependence on dwindling stocks of wood and to explode in the eighteenth century's culmination of the coal-based industrial revolution.

It was the discovery of methods of smelting iron-ore with coal by Abraham Darby in the early eighteenth century which quite literally took the heat out of the Forests. Although the Darbys zealously guarded their secrets they could not keep them for ever and iron-foundries were soon being operated in the Coalbrookdale region by men such as William Reynolds and, across the western bank of the Severn, by 'Iron Jack' Wilkinson with his foundry at nearby Broseley. Coalbrookdale prospered because it was centred not only upon deposits of iron-ore and coal but also upon the Severn which was for long the major outlet for its products. Once the canal system had been built in the latter part of the century to centre upon the Midlands, the way was open for the development of the south Staffordshire coalfield and the Coalbrookdale region was destined to become something of a backwater in the later developments of industrial England.

Of course, the discovery of the Darby process did not mean that all the charcoal burning iron-works of the Weald and the

Forest of Dean automatically ceased production overnight. The iron-masters of the Weald were certainly not conservationists and hung out until they were driven to close down by the spectre of possible bankruptcy. In time coal became cheaper than charcoal, though at the beginning of the eighteenth century, it was still too costly to be transported profitably to the Wealden furnaces. Once coal came to compete as a cheaper fuel than charcoal the Wealden furnaces – faced with transportation costs which the coalfield industries did not have – went rapidly out of business. Gone now were the days of the great Sussex ironmasters such as Peter Farnsden, whose vast ironworks at Sedlescombe had supplied much of the Parliamentary cannon during the Civil War. The smouldering slag heaps ceased to burn and gradually became overgrown. In time descriptions of some Wealden villages, such as Brede and Beckley Furnace as blackened and begrimed hell-holes seemed to belong almost to the realms of fiction. However, it was not until 1828 – more than a century after Darby had discovered his coal smelting process – that the last Wealden ironworks, at Ashburnham, closed down.

It has been said, with some justification, that it was Darby who made the 'Victory' possible, that is, by making the English iron industry independent of timber as its fuel supply, it could be claimed that Darby had a potent hand in creating the circumstances in which there was enough timber for Nelson's flagship and other men o' war and, indirectly in contributing to England's naval supremacy. It is certain that if coal had not come to replace charcoal as the fuel of the iron trades that either all of England's woodland would have disappeared or that the industry would have been so constricted that the industrial revolution could hardly have occurred as an English phenomenon. Charcoal burning had not only cleared wide tracts of the Weald and the Forest of Dean but had left only a remnant of Sherwood and had resulted in the virtual disappearance of the once great forests of Rockingham and Arden. As far as English woodland was concerned the Coalbrookdale ironmasters were indirectly the greatest conservationists it was to know.

The Wealden iron industry ceased to function largely because it lay too far from a coalfield to be able to possess a fuel supply which would permit it to compete economically with the iron industry in the Midlands and the North. Such was not the case with the Forest of Dean which had a coalfield all of its own. Coal had been mined here, though only in small quantities, since at least the fifteenth century. For some decades the local iron industry was to be able to compete with other centres. Gradually, however, it began to decline, not due to any shortage of fuel but because the local supply of iron-ore began to give out. The industry, nonetheless, was to survive into the present century. It was not until 1939 that the last Dean ironstone mine – the New Dunn Mine near Sling – went out of production.

But if the iron industry gradually died in the forest its place was to be taken by coal-mining. The freeminers operated increasingly in larger groups and, by 1900, the Dean coalfield was achieving an output of a million tons *per annum*. This was to bring about a steady increase in the size of the forest population and naturally to swell such villages as Stounton, Micheldean, Coleford and Littledean.

After 1900, however, the industry had passed its boom period. There was a local recession in the trade and it did not really pick up again until the First World War. The original mines, which had been easily worked, were now beginning to be exhausted and the miners met with an increasing number of geological and pumping problems. A large number of pits were closed, though some of the freeminers managed to stay in business.

The decline in coal mining was to some extent offset by a revival of the former quarrying trade and also by the creation of trading estates at Lydney, Coleford and Cinderford. A further factor which has greatly helped to nourish the area in more recent years has been the development of tourism – which has saved more than one industrially derelict area of our countryside.

It is, perhaps, appropriate here to make some small attempt to correct the very general misconception that organized industry virtually began with the eighteenth-century industrial revolution – a process whose hallmarks were the steam engine and the use of coal for iron-smelting, which has variously been estimated as commencing somewhere between

1720 and 1760. Yet many of the constituent elements of this movement were in being at least two centuries before the activities of such men as Darby and Watt.

Even in the Middle Ages it is known that the iron-ore smelting industry of the Forest of Dean became concentrated in the hands of the Malemort family and the monks of Flaxley Abbey. It was something of a natural development for the small forge-owner to be gradually eased out in favour of the large-scale iron-master for, as the industry expanded, it was only the more wealthy owners who could afford the outlay necessary to expand the forge to the point where it became an ironworks and themselves, in consequence, ironmasters. Ironworks came to dominate the industry in the Weald and here, as elsewhere, in the time of Elizabeth I, these at first were in the hands of the aristocracy such as the Dukes of Norfolk. In Derbyshire the Earls of Devonshire also had a number of foundries.

Again, contrary to general belief, this early industry was not entirely charcoal based. Pit coal could be used, at least in the secondary stages. Charcoal was used in the first two stages of the conversion of iron-ore into workable metal, namely in the original blast-furnace and subsequently in the forge which produced the purified iron. Coal however, could be used after these processes, as the impurities had now been removed from the original ore. Thus coal could be used at the chaffery forges which shaped the wrought iron into a form convenient for use by either the smith, the rolling mill or the slitting mills. Coal could also be used by these in their own operations. Thus, while the two early stages of production were located near or in the forests, the later stages tended to move into the coalfield regions. However, as we have seen, this was not to be the case with the Wealden furnaces while the denudation of the remaining woodland of Feckenham and the Staffordshire-Worcestershire border was to some extent brought about by the domestic nailing industry which covered a large area of this part of the Midlands.

It was the nailing industry which led to the rise of the Foleys of Stourbridge as one of England's leading families of ironmasters. Richard Foley was the son of a Dudley nailer who prospered first by selling nails and later by becoming the master of a forge. In 1627 he built a rolling and slitting mill at Stourbridge and ran this in conjunction with a furnace he bought at West Bromwich. His son Thomas later expanded the business and, by 1669, he owned thirteen forges, four slitting mills, four furnaces and a warehouse. Thomas's own sons again expanded the family enterprise with a series of partnerships which gave them control of ironworks in Cheshire, Nottinghamshire, Derbyshire and the Forest of Dean as well as around Stourbridge. By the beginning of the eighteenth century they exercised control over more than forty ironworks and were largely supplying materials for the expanding metal industries of the Black Country and Birmingham.

There were other ironmasters, both in the West Midlands and in other areas, whose organizations much resembled those of the Foleys. The industry was of considerable size by the last decades of the seventeenth century and it was largely its dependence on charcoal in the primary stages of production that limited its growth even further. Once the Darby process became generally known the way was opened for an unprecedented expansion which could not have occurred had not the industry, in almost all other respects, had a long history of development.

Many industries, of course, moved from charcoal to pit coal much earlier than iron manufacture. Glassmaking is a case in point, another industry which tended to concentrate in the west Midland region. In 1418 we find glasshouses being run, appropriately enough, by a John Glasman of Rugeley. Contrary to general belief glass manufacture in this region considerably predates the influx of European Protestant refugees in the late sixteenth century. However, the early industry contributed to the wastage of forest land as did the early kilns for brick and tile making. Local tile making made quite extensive inroads into the Forest of Knaresborough.

It was the increasing shortage of local timber for fuel that led to the increasing import of foreign iron from the time of Elizabeth until the mid eighteenth century. Spanish iron went largely to the furnaces of the Weald while Swedish iron went to establish an iron-industry on the north-east coast. There were ironworks at Sunderland and Winlaton near Newcastle-on-Tyne, at the latter the iron-master Sir Ambrose Crawley having, at the beginning of the eighteenth century, a factory employing more than a thousand workers. This was the largest unit of factory production to predate the steam revolution.

It is generally true that by the beginning of the Tudor period England's industries had largely withered away the primeval forests. The iron industry had been the greatest culprit but many other trades had made their contribution. Things could have hardly gone on this way much longer. By the early sixteenth century London was being seriously hit by a fuel shortage and the future expansion of the capital may have been seriously curtailed if it had not been for the increasing use of 'sea-coal' shipped from the coalfield around Newcastle-on-Tyne. The price of timber was beginning to soar and a writer is found lamenting that timber had risen in price from a penny a load to two shillings "by reason of the iron mills". It was estimated that to smelt one ton of iron it took five thousand cubic feet of timber. With timber costs being what they were it is easy to see why foreign wrought iron was being imported wherever possible.

To conclude this brief survey of forest-based industry it may be said that in late Anglo-Saxon times almost all industries needing fuel for the processing of their raw materials at some stage of production were located in the forests. Five hundred years later this was no longer the case. This was partly because the forests themselves had seen their boundaries pushed back to the point where most industries still relying upon them for fuel now found themselves well outside these boundaries. Also the shortage of timber was leading increasingly to the use of coal wherever possible and to the location of many industries in the region of the nascent coalfields. To my mind it is this use of coal as a primary fuel that marks the real beginning of England's industrial revolution – a process which began largely in the early sixteenth century and culminated, rather than originated, in Darby's Coalbrookdale iron-smelting discovery some two centuries later.

However, there was some small movement against the general trend. As early as the fourteenth century some attempt had been made at conservation in the New Forest to safeguard the saplings which were used in the construction of the daub-and-wattle houses of the time. Later, in Kent and Surrey, some small areas of woodland came to be cultivated to provide poles for use in the hop-yards. The same was true in the area around High Wycombe, where woodland was protected in connection with the growing local furniture trade. In some parts of the country the owners of country houses were, in a small measure, to contribute to reafforestation in planting schemes meant to beautify their estates. But these were ornamental plantations and can hardly be claimed to have have redressed the situation brought about by the charcoal burners.

Nowadays the majority of English woodlands are managed by the Forestry Commission. Timber has long ago ceased to be our basic fuel supply and many traditional uses of timber have now been superceded by other materials. The Commission still, however, supplies pit-props, railways sleepers and materials for the furniture trade. Increasingly however, it is supplying the needs of the domestic building industry as well as the paper and fibreboard trade. However, in what remains of our forestland, there is now a sound policy of replating. It is all a far cry from the days when the smoke of the charcoal burners' fires was rapidly betokening the complete disappearance of English woodland.

5

The Outlaws

The major outlaw legends of the English forests belong to a period beginning roughly toward the end of the twelfth century and ending toward the close of the fourteenth. Many were first set down in the late fifteenth and early sixteenth centuries, although very many had probably existed long before this in ballad form.

There were, of course, earlier outlaws than those of which might be described as of the Robin Hood genre – just as there were to be later ones as well. Two exceptional figures made their names as Anglo-Saxon heroes resisting foreign entrenchmen following the Norman invasion. The story of one, Hereward the Wake, who – sometimes aided by the Danes – engaged in guerilla warfare based on the Fens is generally well-known. However, that of Eadric the Wild, who originally held lands in south Shropshire and whose resistence was based from the forests of Morfe and Clun, is not so well celebrated.

Like Hereward the Wake, Eadric the Wild, or 'Eadric of the Woodland' as he was more commonly known, was a Saxon thegn who had been dispossessed and his lands awarded to Normans, notably to Richard Fitz Scrob. The wooded country gave ample cover for Eadric's 'freedom-fighting' exploits and, by 1069, he was leading a sizable band of adherents against the local Normans.

Richard Fitz Scrob appears as a particular enemy perhaps, apart from the fact that he largely occupied Eadric's inheritance, because he was not one of the conquering Normans who had arrived under William's banner. He was instead one of those 'friends of the Confessor' whom the old king had favoured in an attempt to diminish the power of the

Godwin Earls of Wessex. If it were possible the Saxon landowners hated this breed of Norman with even more venom than they did William's men.

Eadric must have recruited a considerable band of followers for, in 1069, he led a successful attack against Fitz Scrob's fortress of Richard's Castle burning it to the ground. Later he led a more ambitious expedition against the newly erected castle at Shrewsbury. Here he was successful in driving out the Norman garrison and took over the castle himself. Maybe he had some hope of help from the north, for the Saxon earls Morcar and Edwin had not finally surrendered to William and there was still the hope that some part of England would survive to be the kingdom of Edgar the Atheling. But no help was to arrive and Eadric had to withdraw to the woodland when he received news that William was sending an army to retake the castle at Shrewsbury. The Norman presence on the Welsh Border was growing and, although he continued to harry individual strongpoints and supply columns, Eadric now lacked the confidence to mount major attacks against the conquerors.

For a year he lived very largely in the woodland and, in the summer of 1070, was finally captured. He may have expected to die, but William was inclined to mercy. After Eadric had sworn an oath of fealty to the new monarch he was awarded lands on the Welsh border where William no doubt considered he would find ample scope for his fighting spirit. Legends have grown about some of Eadric's exploits – but what is given here are the few brief facts which survive the sifting of the historical sieve.

Robin Hood was far from being the only medieval outlaw to gather around his name a life story that owed far more to legend than to fact. Yet, at the same time, the exploits of the average – and in many cases of the not so average – outlaw were hardly of the type to stray into immortality via the chivalric tradition. From the point of view of most people these exploits were outrages and were best forgotten. Almost certainly the poor fervently wished that a few of the outlaws would take after the idealized Robin Hood and rob from the rich to give to the poor, rather than robbing the poor and giving nothing to anyone. But then, the Robin Hood tradition was, to a great extent, wishful thinking and was hardly written up as a code of behaviour for rural bandits.

One early fourteenth-century outlaw who was certainly to prove he was no Robin Hood was Malcolm Musard. Musard was lord of the Gloucestershire village of Saintbury, also held land at Abbots Morton and Aston Somerville in Worcestershire and was sprung of a family which had been established in England since the time of the Conquest. After rampaging and pillaging throughout the Feckenham Forest region he was to be duly rewarded for his activities by the post of Chief Forester of Feckenham and was later to be appointed Constable of Hanley Castle.

Musard's activities appear to have begun with poaching and he headed a gang, including two of his brothers and the rector of Abbot's Morton, which broke into the part of the Abbot of Westminster at Tiddesley and the park of the Earl of Warwick at Beoley. But Musard seems to have soon tired of these traditional exploits and began to go into the medieval equivalent of the protection racket. Most of his chosen victims seem to have paid up – for Musard headed a formidible outlaw army which at times could be as much as 300 strong. In any case the medieval legal process was a slow affair and, as juries could often be bribed and intimidated, it was by no means certain that justice would prevail.

Musard also seems to have hired out some or all of his gang at various times to add a little weight to one side or another in a particularly vexatious local dispute. Musard's men were responsible for a whole series of beatings up in the region. Occasionally Musard's methods did not work. He attempted to gain a protection payment from Thomas of Lench and when this was refused he arranged to pasture cattle on Lench's land at Rous Lench and sent down a gang which felled 200 oaks in Lench's wood. It is not known if Thomas of Lench still refused payment after this calamity. The rector of Martley obviously feared the same treatment and paid Musard ten quarterns of wheat for the sake of peace and quiet.

It was not until the following year – 1305 – that Musard was called upon to answer for his activities by the Serriff of Worcestershire. Naturally enough he and his associates preferred to ignore the call and, after a suitable time had elapsed, they were duly declared to be outlaws. Musard now appears to have decided to develop the 'rent-a-gang' side of his business and undertook a commission from Godfrey of Crombe – who had been evicted from the Gloucestershire living of Weston-sub-Edge by the Bishop of Worcester – to get rid of his replacement, one Thomas of Weston. Godfrey's action in recruiting Musard was an act of pure revenge, for he could not have hoped to gain back by violence alone. At the head of a gang provided by Musard he arrived at Weston where the gang broke into the rector's house carrying off his grain and other goods. The gang then went onto the house of the lord of the manor, Sir John Giffard, where they peppered both the house and the manor servants with their bows and arrows.

But Godfrey of Crombe obviously thought he had not gone far enough. A month later he was back, this time in the company of Musard himself, Musard's two brothers William and Ralph, Geoffrey of Saintsbury the rector of Abbot's Morton and Musard's leading lieutenant, Hugh of Wardington. The raiding party came on horseback, armed with lances as well as with bows and arrows. The action of the previous month was repeated, though this time the rector's house was severely damage and his fishponds were broken up. Thomas of Weston seems to have known what was going to happen for he left the village before the raiders appeared.

Musard was to be eventually brought to book for this and other crimes. But he had influential friends and relatives. In 1307 he was found innocent of all the charges brought against him at the Sherriff's court at Worcester. However, it appears very unlikely that everything he was accused of was the work of imagination or malice.

When he became Chief Forester of Feckenham his career went on much as before, often in association with the freebooting rectors of Abbot's Morton and Aston Somerville. With people like Musard in charge of the royal administration of the forests the Crown had little hope of seeing but a small proportion of the actual revenue and no hope at all that they would be well managed.

Robin Hood may or may not have been an actual person. Even if he did exist his accredited exploits are probably almost all fable while those that have their foundation in fact were equally probably the work of others. However, there were many outlaws in the Middle Ages whose exploits were so like those of the legendary Robin as to create an inevitable parallel. One such was Piers Venables of Derbyshire who was referred to in a petition to Parliament in 1439 as having rescued a prisoner being taken to Tutbury Castle. It was stated that he had gathered around him a gang of men "beyng of his clothing, and in manere of insurrection wente into the woodes in that country like it hadde be Robyn Hode and his meynee".

Derbyshire suffered particularly from the presence of outlaw bands, especially, in the fourteenth century, from the activities of one led by James Coterel who, like Malcolm Musard, was a member of the gentry class. The Coterel gang was quite as wild as that led by Musard, calling themselves "the society of savage men" and specializing in the business of extortion.

Outlaws of this category often went in for titles of rank, aping the organization of noble society. Gang leaders were often referred to as 'Captain' and one operating near York styled himself "Lionell, King of the Rout of Raveners". Some even claimed to have set up a legal system of their own in opposition to that of the Crown. In the Forest of Knaresborough William Beckwith and his accomplices established their own Parliament, the Dodelowe, which claimed to sanction the appointment of local officials. In Essex the outlaw gangs were at times so strong as to make the operation of the law of the Crown impossible. In many ways all this is vaguely reminiscent of Robin Hood's court under the "greenwood tree". Yet assemblies which were to be described by royal officials as leading to "the subversion of the law, the oppression of the people, dishonour of the duke (of Lancaster) and the loss of his servants' lives", cannot be said to have any place in the popular ballad tradition.

Yet in some ways Robin had a respectable lineage. In the late thirteenth century Sherwood threw up someone who may even have been the original Robin Hood. This was Roger Godberd, a former adherent of de Montfort in the baron's war, who took to the forest in protest against the rather unsympathetic terms of his pardon. Godberd's reign of terror was relatively brief, but he seems to have robbed and killed a large number of travellers before his capture. This came as the result of a Crown commission specially appointed to track him down – something which took the commissioners no less than four years. The Coterel gang also operated in Sherwood Forest and, to put a strange twist into the outlaw story, had as one of their allies Richard Ingram, who was a number of times Sherriff of Nottingham. But it was not the normal scene of their activities.

Although most outlaw bands were relatively small in number some were extremely large and more resembled private armies. In the Forest of Knaresborough William Beckwith headed a gang which, in 1392, numbered in the region of 500 men and was said to have previously been even larger. Operating from the forest land of Essex the gang of John FitzWalter was large enough to be able to lay siege to Colchester for more than two months, and the siege was only raised when the townfolk paid FitzWalter £40. Obviously when outlaw gangs began to operate on this sort of scale, the area in which they were based was virtually under their control. It was pointless to evoke the law in such circumstances as friends and bribed or intimidated juries would almost always ensure that they escaped any charges.

For periods of time ranging sometimes up to two, three, or four years large parts of the countryside became quite literally gang-land. On the face of it it would seem that the Crown would have found it extremely difficult to re-establish its authority in such regions. That it did so with apparent ease was largely due to the fact that the leaders of most of the outlaw bands were members of the gentry class, whose outlaw exploits were often at bottom motivated by feelings of revenge. Such feelings may have had their origin in certain men considering they had been slighted and not given sufficient power in the social heirarchy. Some outlaw leaders were younger sons, dispossessed by complicated laws of inheritance, or men whose life of crime had originated in a local land feud.

Even if the outlaws could rarely be brought to justice the Crown evolved a way of dealing with them in the form of the sale of pardons, which in itself amounted to a fine. Normally such a sale would be accompanied by a promise to appoint a former outlaw leader to local office. As this was very often what he had really wanted in the first place the arrangement often worked quite well. The sale of the pardon paid for the outlaw's crimes – at least as far as the Crown was concerned – and the reward of office generally guaranteed that the former outlaw leader no longer led his band in acts of pillage. Local peace was therefore maintained and an outlaw transformed into a royal official.

There were other ways of gaining pardons too. Occasionally, for largely political reasons, the Crown would grant a general pardon. At such a time a pardon could be purchased for a few shillings rather than the hundreds of pounds an individual pardon could cost at other times. Then again pardons could also be obtained by those who had performed military service for the king. It is not without significance that so many members of the outlaw bands undertook service in the border campaigns.

Mention has been made in an earlier chapter of the maladministration of Feckenham Forest by its royal officials. The situation was certainly not without parallel. In the Forest of Dean the royal officials seem to have been even more predatory than those of Feckenham. Perhaps this was because so many of them were drawn from noble families such as the Clares and Beauchamps who – out of the eyes of the Crown – had long been accustomed to doing as they liked with any land they administered. The Dean foresters seem to have made a profit out of everything to be found in the forest – with the exception of the deer with which it can only be presumed they were not interested.

Large areas of the Dean woodlands were converted to arable – at a fee. The common lands were overstocked with pigs, sheep and cattle and foresters felled and sold vast amounts of timber. The activities we have noted in Feckhenham were to be repeated in Dean on an even larger scale. In fact it becomes fairly clear that, though they were supposed to ensure the implementation of the Laws of Forest, the royal officials generally regarded their offices as little more than a means whereby to amass a personal fortune. It has been estimated that, in some years, the king was lucky to receive a third of the revenue collected for the Crown in Dean. Embezzlement on this scale makes the officials into greater thieves than the outlaw gangs themselves.

However, the frauds practised by the forest officials have only been mentioned here to demonstrate that those charged with the hunting down of the outlaws were very often little better than their quarry. In fact, a broad streak of lawlessness and criminality ran through almost every reach of medieval society. One of the major reasons why so many of the outlaw gangs were never brought to justice was because local officials were often quite willing to do a deal with outlaw leaders – which often amounted to their giving the outlaws a franchise to operate in a certain part of the country in return for a share of any takings.

Yet this sort of arrangement would have applied mainly to the larger gangs and particularly to those gangs whose leaders had social connections with those charged with administering royal justice. It would hardly seem that such an arrangement operated on behalf of the lowly born gang that plied its trade at the Trimperley Pass at the beginning of the fourteenth century. The Trimperley Pass lies just beyond Bewdley and was a favourite route for merchants returning to the South and Midlands from the fairs and markets of the North Welsh Border. In a series of ambushes the gang waylaid a large number of merchants here. But it proved almost impossible to capture the gang, and even when one member was eventually brought to justice, he managed to avoid the full consequences of the charges brought against him.

The captured man was William of Nonnechurch who was tried at Worcester and declared guilty. But William was a cleric and succeeded in evading the juridiction of the court by seeking 'benefit of clergy'. This meant that the case was passed to the local ecclesiastical court. Ecclesiastical courts could not apply the death sentence and, in general, their treatment of offenders was far less severe than was the case with the secular courts. At the same time that William was managing to avoid the full consequences of his actions u related case being brought against Felicia la Nywemannes. She came from Kingsford, a few miles west of Trimperley, and

Woodland solitude. The forest as perhaps it could be seen in the mind's eye

Sherwood Forest:
the Major Oak

Silver birch

The Border Forest: sheep and lambs grazing near piles of pit props against a background of conifer forest. But the needs of the hill farmer and the forester are often at variance

The yew—once of religious significance. In later times cherished by England's bowmen

A Forestry Commission fire tower. Fire is an ever present danger in forest areas, especially in the summer months

it was alleged that she had kept the outlaw gang supplied with food and drink. Just what happened to this Severnside Maid Marian is not known, but it is quite likely that William of Nonnechurch had informed against her.

It is perhaps, surprising to find so many members of the clergy involved in banditry. William of Nonnechurch and the clerics who rode with Malcolm Musard on his hell-raising jaunts were far from being the only members of the cloth to be involved in the outlaw game. In the Forest of Arden in the late thirteenth century – when there was still some woodland left – one Joan of Audeshale was attacked by what amounted to a small clerical detachment. She was robbed, then locked up in the old de Montfort castle of Beaudesert at Henley-in-Arden. When she was finally released she was to accuse the rector of Preston Bagot, Peter of Leicester, of organizing the whole affair. Peter of Leicester, however, appears to have got away with the offence – probably because he was on good terms with the jurymen.

But not all robberies in the forest were committed by gangs of outlaws. Often, it would seem, they were isolated instances when a group of local men – otherwise well-respected in their region – just do not seem to have been capable of resisting the temptation to rob a group of particularly wealthy travellers. One such incident took place on Cannock Chase in February 1341. Two merchants, William Drakelowe and Richard Horninglowe, accompanied by their servant were taking two horses laden with spices and textiles worth £40 to a market to be held at Stafford. On the fringe of the chase they were intercepted by Sir Robert Rideware and two of his followers who took the two merchants captive, though the servant managed to escape. The merchants were taken to Lapley Priory where more of Sir Richard's followers and friends had gathered. Here the plunder was divided.

The robbers now took their captives to Blythelry Priory, claiming to be retainers of the king and demanding admittance on this account. But the prioress had her suspicions and refused them admission. However, Rideware and his men were undeterred by this. They forced their way into the priory and broke open the outhouses for fodder for their horses.

However, the merchants' servant had been busy. He had followed the robbers to the priory and returned the following morning in the company of the king's bailiff from Lichfield and a posse of the townsfolk. The bailiff called upon Rideware to surrender. A short fight took place and Rideware's party fled, some of them being killed in the pursuit. Eventually the bailiff's party gave up further pursuit and began to move back toward Lichfield.

They were still in the chase when they were overtaken by Rideware and his men who had now been reinforced by others led by a kinsman, Sir Walter Rideware, lord of the manor of Hamstall Rideware. The bailiff's men were caught off-guard and the booty was recaptured. When Drakelowe and Honninglowe later went to present their complaint at Stafford they found Rideware's men manning the town gates and could not gain entrance. Ultimately they complained to the Earl of Arundel at Lichfield – though just what was the eventual outcome of this episode is not recorded. However it would seem that this exploit, which began essentially as a minor affair, was one that got out of hand. Once it did, the Ridewares are seen making strenuous efforts to prevent it going any further.

This is a long way from the traditional idea of Robin Hood and his men. It seems a little pointless to consider if there were really any 'good' outlaws at all. On the face of it, there were not. There may, of course, have been the occasional chivalric incident – but bad only shows up as good when compared to real evil. But it is worth remembering that the English peasantry considered the Norman aristocracy as hated conquerors well into the fourteenth century. Almost anything that gave annoyance to their overlords would have engaged their sympathy.

Yet, greenwood banditry was not a chivalric art and obeyed no chivalric code. It was, instead, almost to be classed among the ranks of medieval professions and was conducted with near complete ruthlessness. There are a number of accounts of women and children being killed in outlaw raids – one even comes from a tale of Robin Hood himself – but it should not be thought that the outlaws were cold-blooded murderers as well. The outlaw profession demanded secrecy and women and children were occasionally killed to ensure it.

Robin Hood apart, the medieval woodlands were full of legends, many very ancient. Many of these had their origin in the misted world of the Celt rather in that of the Saxon English. Puck and less benign spirits of the old religion lingered in the English forests. In the wooded depths of Malvern Chase it was the Celtic past that was responsible for the legend of Ragged Stone Hill. The shadow cast by the hill spread across the chase at sunset and it was believed that it brought death to anyone it touched. It was a belief that seemed to hark back to days when the hill had once been the site of ritual sacrifice. In Dean was a somewhat more explicable legend, again associated with the onset of nightfall. this told of the silent ghosts of boys of an unearthly whiteness, rising naked through the ground at the feet of a forest miner on his homeward trek to bear him downward with them into the ground. These were said to be the spirits of children killed in the mine-workings of the forest. It can only be said that many miners did lose their lives blundering into abandoned shafts. If the legend contained little actual fact it was at least valid as a cautionary tale. On the subject of children the New Forest seems to claim an English version of the Pied Piper of Hamelin. However, I rather doubt if it is really much more than an adaptation of the German story – for it does not seem to have been recorded until the mid-nineteenth century. The details differ little from the German original, except that they take place at Newtown. Being cheated out of his fee the piper entrances the village children with his music and, leading them through the streets of the town, fimally disappears with them into the heart of the forest. However, at least there remains no unhappy cripple child.

The 'babes-in-the-wood' legend crops up all over the place – and still forms a staple pantomime subject. Often it was not a legend at all, for unwanted children were all too often left in the forest where their death from exposure of starvation was a near certainty. I quote one instance from the eighteenth century. Here a father had died at Beverely in Yorkshire leaving his infant daughter in the care of his brother. The brother wished to claim the family estate and took the child into the nearby woodland, hiding it in a hollow tree. Two days later it was discovered by two hunters, still alive but having gnawed at its own flesh. The uncle had arranged for the burial of a wax effigy of the child, with an elaborate funeral. The effigy was now exhumed. It is said that the uncle was later tried at York Assizes. However, there would appear to be no record of this.

However, it is the tales of Robin Hood which have largely survived from the times when the forests were the haunts of thieves, cut-throats and the dispensers of assorted mayhem. Many of the Robin Hood legends have him as the dispossessed and banished Earl of Huntingdom – a doubtful assertion as this title was for long held by the Princes of Powys and passed into abeyance in the fourteenth century. Maid Marian was likewise enobled as the daughter of the Norman Lord FitzWalter – though just how she came to be camping out in the greenwood is never satisfactorily explained.

One legend asserts that Robin and Marian had a pair of rivals for his physical prowess and her beauty. These were George-a-Green, the pinder of Wakefield and Beatrice, daughter of Justice Grymes and known as 'the flower of the North'. At this point it is fitting to explain that a pinder was one in charge of the pinfold or pound and was responsible for the rounding up of stray sheep and cattle. The upshot of the claims of George and Beatrice was that Robin and Marian, together with Friar Tuck, Scathlock and Little John journeyed to Wakefield to put George and Beatrice to the test. Wakefield, by the way, is one of those places where there is known to have existed a Robin Hud – though whether this was in fact the outlaw of legend no one can say.

The pinder ultimately fought Robin and his men not as the result of an open challenge, but because he caught them riding their horses across growing crops – and it was one of his duties to prevent such thoughtless occurrences. Scathlock and Little John he defeated quite easily with his quarter-staff and Friar Tuck, despite his reputation, did not present him with much greater difficulty. However, as was to be expected, Robin Hood, proved more difficult to overcome. But the pinder, who had no idea of his contestant's identity, regarded him as just one more scoundrel in need of a sharp lesson. He took a little longer in pursuading Robin to submit but, the tale is at pains to stress, not much longer. Sprawled in the field Robin now declared who he was. The pinder replied that after King Richard, Robin was the man he most admired. Marian, not to be outdone by Robin's defeat, now maintained that Beatrice was truly 'the flower of the North'. After much ale and roast beef Robin and Marian leave this particular tale occupying an unaccustomed second-place. In fact, in quite a few tales, Robin comes off worst and some contain an obvious 'anti-Robin' element. A number treat him more as a woodland gangster than as a folk-hero.

Robin was far from being regarded as a universal dispenser of gentle thoughts and other people's money. He was also seen as the archetypal boaster, the bar-room boor and braggart whose hyperbolic exploits taxed not only the patience but the credulity of the average man. Not for nothing was a boaster often brought to heel with the taunt 'turn again Robin Hood' – a medieval turn of phrase approximating to 'pull the other one'.

Some authorities would maintain that Robin was far more than a mortal man. The flimsy evidence for his existence when compared to the very substantial figure portrayed in the tales and ballads has aroused the interest of anthropologists. These have attempted to explain Robin's place in English folk-lore not in terms of the social history of the late Middle Ages but in terms of him being a late representative of old Saxon, Norse and Celtic beliefs.

Robin has been equated with the ancient sun-god, the Sheriff of Nottingham with the traditional winter king and the whole corpus of Robin Hood tales, because they identify reasonably closely with the seasons, has been said to be the shadow of an ancient fertility cult. Robin Hood has been associated with the famous wood-spirit Robin Goodfellow and much made of the probability that Robin Hood and his Fellowship seem both an extension and a corruption of the name. It is also pointed out that in certain West-Midland shires words prefixed by a 'w' often lose it in pronunciation. Woden – the old Norse god – would thus have been pronounced in those parts as 'oden' or 'ooden' and Hood could be a corruption of this. Again, staying with the Northern gods, there was a Teutonic wood spirit known as

Hudekin, who could also be connected philologically to the name Hood. However, if we stay with rural West-Midland pronunciation it would be well to remember that 'wood' is pronounced as 'ood' even to this day. Robin Hood could thus be simply 'Robin of the Wood' via 'Robin a 'ood' to Robin Hood. Speculation as to the origin of the name could be endless.

It has been said that the tale of Robin's death at Kirklees Priory represents the symbolic sacrifice of a victim representing the sun-god to the spirit of winter. Thus this part of the story would be linked to mythology connected with the eternal conflict of the seasons. It is said that Robin as sun-god knew he was bound for death on his journey to the priory. This interpretation claims this is evident in his passing the mourning women on his way to the priory and in the witch – as a represientive of the old religion – 'banning' him at the black water.

Robin is also found associated with many May-Day festivals and, especially with the Morris Dance. The germ of the Robin and Marian connection with these plays and dances seems to come from twelfth-century France where a story told of how Robin rescued his love Marion from the advances of a lustful knight. The similarity of the names of the French and English pair has been enough for it to be suggested that Robin is a traditional pagan figure whose activities have been preserved in the drama associated with seasonal rural celebrations.

The possibility that Robin may have a pagan past has been further related to the existence of many natural features named after him, in the form of chairs, stones, butts and barrows. It is pointed out that only someone with a long life in traditional myth could be expected to leave such a widely dispersed topographical heritage behind him.

With the exception of the last assertion all of this many have some basis in fact. However, if Robin Hood was some kind of relative to, or representative of Robin Goodfellow and his spiritual like he was also far more than this. Even if we are to see in him some vestige of a mythological sun-god, he also, and far more forcibly, is portrayed as a man of his time. Perhaps there is something in the theory that links the outlaw bands' livery of Lincoln green to the colour of summer and new growth. But there is perhaps more to be said that green clothing would have been a very good form of camouflage in the greenwood and at least the Venables gang are on record as having used it in the early fifteenth century.

The connection with Hudekin does sound a possibility – though it is very much to be doubted that the medieval ballad makers knew of it. They were concerned to appeal to the popular audience of the day and decked Robin out as a pastoral hero against corrupt justice not as a cross between Peter Pan and some blood-steeped Scandinavian demon. Some of the savagery in the early ballads may owe something to a lingering memory of gory Norse mythology. But medieval England was also a place of great violence. Whatever their ultimate derivations it seems more correct to regard the ballads as a mirror to the times in which they were written than as shadows of earlier symbolism. A few incidents in the Robin-Hood story may stand up to scrutiny from a mythological point of view. But this can hardly be a reason to say that the whole of the story has a mythological origin. Medieval story-tellers had a habit of borrowing material from elsewhere and incorporating it in their own work for the sake of effect. It may have seemed a good idea to introduce a witch and some mourning women to give the tale added impact. Very conceivably these two elements played no part in the original tale. However, we have no way of telling this for certain. The matter must remain an open question.

It is reasonably certain that Marian was a late addition to the greenwood tales. The early ballads make no mention of her. It would seem that her connection with the story came about as a confusion between the English tales of Robin Hood and the French tales of Robin and Marion. The Morris Dance, with which the two figures were so closely identified, came from abroad probably not earlier than the fourteenth century. Thus, when looking for the genesis of Robin Hood, it is first necessary to separate the English from the French strands of the tale. This is now so interwoven as to be impossible to achieve with certainty.

From a mythological and anthropological standpoint we are left with a long series of possibilities – few of which can be decried, but many of which have little relevance if we are concerned to see the medieval outlaw as a figure of his time. If Maid Marian is an importation from France then she antedates most of the rest of the greenwood brotherhood and her links with Robin Hood, Little John and the rest have been forged by imaginative ballad makers rather than by factual circumstance. One could speculate on what may have fired the imaginations of these anonymous men – but the sensible answer would appear to lie in their desire to tell a good story rather than to delve into mythological allegories about which they were almost certainly completely ignorant.

Largely because of the paucity of evidence most theories advanced concerning Robin and his band would seem to have some credence. But in general it would seem safe to assume that Robin – irrespective of esoteric origins – emerges foremost as a representative of the late-medieval common man engaged in an endless battle for intrinsic rather than formulated and manipulated justice. Medieval records reveal that not all his exploits were wishful thinking on the part of the ballad makers. All too often their like took place in fact.

Outlawry based upon the forests was not unrelated to periods of general unrest in the England countryside. Roaming bands of brigands certainly came to infest the countryside as soldiers returned home to unemployment after the campaigns of the Hundred Years' War. Added to this, English society in the later Middle Ages was seriously disturbed by two very different calamities in the form of the Black Death and the Peasant's Revolt. When the Wars of the Roses threw the leaders of society at each others' throats in a conflict that raged for much of the fifteenth century it must have seemed to many that society was breaking down completely.

In such circumstances as these it became necessary for a successful outlaw to enter into competition with his rivals armed not only with bow, arrow and quarterstaff but with a good gimmick as well. One such was Richard Stafford who, in the early fourteenth century, based himself upon the woodland of the Weald. Stafford was a former cleric whose ample proportions well fitted him to adopt the pseudonym of 'Frere Tuk'.

Richard Stafford did very little that would give the ballad

makers further scope for elaboration upon the chivalric fables of 'gentle Robin' and his may-time merry men. He began in a modest enough way as the head of a poaching gang undertaking most of their activities in Surrey where the Wealden waste was still sufficiently wooded to offer effective cover whenever danger threatened. But this latter-day Friar Tuk was soon to expand the range of his activities to cover, amongst other things, armed robbery, kidnapping and murder. The kidnapping of children seems to have been a peculiarity of the Tuk gang. It seems to have been undertaken largely for ransom, but perhaps it was also a means of press-ganging recruits. At all events there is the story of a boy who managed to escape from the clutches of the gang. There is no mention that he was being held for ransom and it would seem that he was being kept in the woodland purely to serve the will of the gang. It is not evident that he had taken part in any of the gang's exploits and probably had not because it had been feared that he would only take the opportunity to escape.

Tuk and his maurauders had already been operating for some years when, in 1416, the local authorities made some attempt to bring them to justice. In that year a commission was issued to Thomas Conoys, John Pelham and Thomas Poynyngs "to arrest one assuming the name of Frere Tuck and other evil doers of his retinue who have committed divers murders, homicides, robberies and depredations, etc., in the Counties of Surrey and Sussex and bring them before the King and Council".

As was largely to be expected the commission was a dismal failure. Tuk and his band took to the heath and woodland where no pursuit was possible and after weeks of beating about in the bushes the commissioners apparently gave up their task and went home.

The following year a second attempt was made. A new commission was made, this time in the persons of Robert Hull and William Lasyngley, the previous three having either lost heart or being considered too half-hearted in their efforts.

By now Frere Tuk had widened the area of his activities. The Surrey Weald had become a base from which he led expeditions over an ever-widening territory and his outlaws were pillaging as near to London as Cobham. The two commissioners were instructed to "enquire into the report that a certain person assuming the unusual name of Frere Tuk and other evil doers have entered the parks, warrens and chases of divers leiges of the king in the County of Surrey at divers times, hunted therein and carried off deer, hares, rabbits, pheasants and partridges, burned the houses and lodges for the keeping of the parks and threatened the keepers". It is rather strange that this commission mentions only the poaching activities of the gang and ignores its other crimes.

This second commission was to prove as futile as the first. Tuk and his associates remained uncaught, though the hunt was evidently a hot one, for it was from this time that they moved their activities somewhat westward and began pillaging into neighbouring Hampshire.

The corpulent cleric was never to be brought to justice. He lived in the Wealden greenwood until 1429 maintaining himself and his followers by a profitable life of poaching and robbery. All attempts to capture him were finally abandoned and he ultimately bought himself back into society by the purchase of a royal pardon. There was little that could have been claimed as noble or romantic in Tuk's career and his life was probably far more the average outlaw pattern than that popularized by the majority of the greenwood ballads.

A determined outlaw band, which was not to be lured by the prospect of pardon, was almost impossible to apprehend. Apart from the royal army there existed no national law-enforcement body and what policing there was existed only on a local basis. If pursuit became too hot wrongdoers had only to take themselves into the next town or county to avoid capture, for the jurisdiction of most county administrations stopped at their own boundaries. This was a matter which was to be only partly solved by the creation of the Bow Street Runners and was not finally concluded until the establishment of a national system of policing in the mid nineteenth century.

In Elizabethan times lawlessness declined, at least when compared to former centuries. Largely absent from Elizabethan records are outlaws of noble birth – after the aristocratic fratricide of the Wars of the Roses the lawless nobles of old were largely figures of the past. Banditry was no longer the recourse of the aggrieved patrician and was stripped of the last shreds of its doubtful glory.

The Elizabethans were as much in love with the printed word as is the modern housewife with her array of kitchen gadgets, for printing was still new enough to posess something of a novelty value. Publications appeared on a host of different subjects from witchcraft to agricultural improvement. A number appeared on the art of the villain and one, John Audley's *Fraternity of the Vagabond* published in 1561, showed that at least one branch of the outlaw tradition was still very much alive. Audley attempted to categorize the various types of vagabond, the genuinely destitute being described as "beggerly", the more vicious as "ruffling". A ruffler was described as "one who goeth with a weapon to seek service, saying he hath been a servitor in the wars, and beggeth for his relief. But his chiefest trade is to rob poor wayfaring men and market women." There were many gradations of ruffler who together formed a large element of the Elizabethan underworld. The slang of the Elizabethan wandering rogue referred to the woodland in which so many sought refuge as "the ruffmans" – from the point of view of the traveller this must often have been a particularly appropriate term.

In the seventeenth and eighteenth centuries the remaining heaths and woodlands of the forest areas were to linger on as the refugees of outlaws – now to be updated to highwaymen and footpads. The Forest of Dean – as early as the post-Restoration years, was said to be over-run by bandits and much the same sort of thing was said of other forest areas including the New Forest and Epping. Epping came in for a considerable amount of attention as it lay so near to London and formed a perfect haven for such famous figures as Dick Turpin and Little Johnny' Sprigg. The latter of these was said to have been comemmorated by the doggerel: "There was a little man and he had a little gun and his bullets were made of lead". Sprigg himself came to a violent end and a house on Palmer's Hill was named after him as Sprigg's Oak, being built on the spot where he was shot and hanged.

Some of the highwaymen, particularly the earlier versions of the breed, may have had some claims to be true 'gentlemen of the road', stealing only from the rich, at least not ill-treating the poor and showing courtesy to ladies of noble birth. These early masked riders were often disposessed men of noble blood, who had lost their lands at the Restoration or – as was often the case – had failed to be restored to those taken from them under the Commonwealth. In the eighteenth century it was Claude Duval who was to continue the tradition of the courtly robber.

The activities of highwaymen in the Epping area led to the establishment of two mounted road patrols which kept their duty station at the Bell Inn on Bell Common. Although these patrols were never completely successful in stamping out highway robbery in the area they were by no means ineffective and over the years their presence was a factor in the decline of the number of crimes committed on the road.

Highwaymen in Epping and elsewhere often went by picturesque names. 'Sixteen String' Jack Rann, however, was only so called after his execution at Tyburn, for on his way to meet the hangman he wore sixteen coloured strings on his garters. For many years he and his gang had plied a ruthless trade along the Essex roads. Few of his victims would have had call to describe him with such a picturesque phrase. A notorious gang, who apparently had no real leader, were the Waltham Blacks who wore masks over blackened faces. They lived in a collection of huts in the Wake valley area of the forest and were so numerous that when their hideout was finally discovered it took a large party of soldiers to break them up. The highwaymen obviously engaged in a profitable business, though they didn't always win outright. In the late eighteenth century a party of seven 'men of the road' held up a stagecoach in the forest and the driver killed three with his blunderbuss – proving that this weapon was far from being the ineffective instrument of popular legend – before he himself was killed by a pistol shot.

Contrary to general belief Dick Turpin also operated very largely with a gang – though he did undertake a number of exploits on his own. The gang was no better than any other and just how Turpin has managed to acquire the reputation of a 'gentleman', robbing with some semblance of civility, must remain something of a mystery. Certainly there is nothing that can be called gentlemanly in the fact that he once roasted an old lady of Laughton over her own fire until she was forced to reveal the hiding place of her money. The story is probably quite true and many Laughton people took to fitting 'Turpin traps' – heavy baulks of timber – at the head of their stairs to prevent Turpin from gaining access to their bedrooms. In fact, in the early eighteenth century, highwaymen and robbers of all sorts were so general in the area that Epping forest folk lived in a constant state of terror.

But Turpin's days were numbered. Even before his execution at York in 1739 he had come very near to being captured in Essex. Today the Turpin's Cave Inn stands on the site of the forest cave that was said to be his hideout and to which he was once tracked down. When challenged he shot his way out to freedom, killing one of his pursuers during the course of his escape.

From this time, however, Turpin's activities in Epping declined for most of his gang was now dispersed, and not long afterward he is found making his famous ride to York. A few memorable exploits on the road sufficed to turn Turpin into a legend in his own lifetime. Yet Turpin was not so much a romantic hero of the road as a burglar, poacher, deer, sheep and cattle thief. Half in acknowledgement of this as much adulation has gone to Black Bess as to Turpin himself, though his famous ride to York must still rank as an epic achievement.

At the time that Turpin met his end the reign of the highwayman was far from being dead. It was to enjoy a fitful existence for the remainder of the eighteenth century and it was still more than a passing adventure to set out in a coach that had to cross through any isolated region, though those around London, such as Hounslow Heath, were with justification the most dreaded.

Yet some highwaymen were still capable of investing at least some of their exploits with the spirit of the Robin Hood of legend. It was a late eighteenth-century highwayman, William Stallard, living at the Upper Perlieu, who was said to have led the Dean foresters in the popular rising known as the 'Bread Riots' in 1795. These included attacks on local flour mills and on carriers taking corn to Gloucester. The *Gloucester Journal* recorded one such attack as follows:

> On Saturday morning, 30th October 1795, as Mr King's waggon, of Bolitree, was bringing a load of barley to the Gloucester Market, it was beset by a number of colliers from the Forest of Dean near the Lea Line, who inquired what the bags contained, and when told it was barley, they cut the bags to examine: whilst this was passing, a waggon, loaded with wheat, came up the hull belonging to Mr Dobson of Harthill, in the parish of Weston, which was taken to in the same manner, and both waggons with the grain were taken off to a place in the Forest of Dean, called Drybrook, where the people divided the corn, and sent back the waggons and horses to the owners.

The Dean foresters, who were experiencing a time of great local suffering because of the failure of successive harvests, regarded Stallard as a local hero. But Stallard's career as an angel of mercy was short-lived. He returned to more profitable pursuits and was ultimately hanged at Gloucester five years later for horse-stealing.

But Stallard was 'on the road' at the end of the era of the English highwaymen. The 'gentlemen' were finding it increasingly difficult to make a living as the nineteenth century dawned. The Bow Street Runners, local road patrols like those in Epping and, later the creation of local constabularies, all made life difficult for the highwayman. Added to this was the fact the coaches now moved much more quickly, especially on the major highways. This was due to a combination of improved road surfaces due to the efforts of such men as Telford and MacAdam, improved coach design, and a greater emphasis on speed by the passenger carrying companies faced with the tight-scheduled competition of the mail-coaches. The ground between Hounslow and Staines, for instance, could be covered at speeds in the region of thirteen miles per hour which, though it certainly did not outpace the highwayman, added greatly to his risks in attempting a hold-up. The highwayman was already a dying breed by the time the railways came to drive him from the roads forever. Once lines were opened throughout the country the highwayman became as redundant as the stage-coaches on which he once had preyed.

In Epping the last person to be held up on the road was a Mr Winder, the father of a local solicitor. One morning in

1837, as he was driving to London, he was stopped by three armed men who demanded his cash and valuables. He handed them over and the men took to the cover of the forest. Mr Winder now drove back to inform the road patrol who set out in pursuit and eventually tracked down the men. A chase ensued and the robbers were finally captured in Whitechapel. One man, who was also wanted for other crimes, was hanged, one was sentenced to penal servitude for life and one got off.

Amongst the many other changes it was to effect, it could be claimed that the advent of the steam locomotive indirectly contributed to making the public highway a far less lawless place than it had been in former times.

6

Iron Men and Wooden Walls

It has been argued that England's iron industry could have continued to expand throughout the seventeenth and eighteenth centuries in both the absence of coal and without seriously depleting the native woodlands any further. But, while England certainly did continue to possess an iron industry, there are many doubts to be raised as to whether, overall, it was an expanding one. Certain sections of the industry did expand, but these were largely the finishing processes such as the chaffery forges where metal that had already been smelted was worked up into usable material using coal as fuel – as the wrought metal had already been rendered free of impurities. The number of iron-slitting mills also increased – but these were largely dependent upon water power. The metal trades themselves proliferated – especially the West-Midland nailing manufacture – but these too could use coal just as effectively as charcoal. One reason for the seventeenth-century opening up of both the Worcestershire Avon and the Stour by 'navigations' was to bring coal from the Forest of Dean and Shropshire to the forges and workshops of the area.

The importation – from the early sixteenth century onward – of pre-worked iron from Spain and Sweden clearly shows where the English weakness lay. An increasing shortage of native timber had so forced up the price of charcoal that it was now cheaper to use pre-worked foreign iron than that produced in England. What prevented the complete closure of the English ironsmelting industry was nothing whatsoever to do with quality but purely the considerations of transport costs. Spanish ore penetrated the Weald largely via the Medway and the Wey Navigation which extended into Surrey as far as Godalming. Swedish ore led to the establishment of an iron industry on the North-east coast effecting the first real shift of the industry to the north of England. Had England's woodlands still been able to provide fully for the needs of the charcoal burning smelters it is unlikely that Swedish ore would ever have come to the North-east and the smelting industry would have remained largely located in its old forest centres.

Despite increasingly adverse conditions local iron-ore processing persisted in the Forest of Dean and the Weald for some time. However, by the end of the seventeenth century, there were no ironworks operating in the Dean Crown woodlands. The Wealden industry was still in fitful business at this time but it, too, was doomed to extinction. Although it had its own iron-ore deposits local timber rose steadily in price, its transportation costs for foreign ore were greater than those of the North-east industry and, as it did not itself lie on a coalfield, the cost of bringing in coal first as a secondary fuel and later as a primary one, rendered the industry increasingly uneconomic when compared to its competitors.

Prior to the introduction of the coal smelting process there were three major factors which contributed toward a gradual reversal of the trend which had led to the virtual disappearance of England's once extensive woodland cover. Foremost was a quickening of Crown and government interest in the extension of the eroded Royal Forests in the interests of providing timber for the Royal Navy. As Secretary to the Admiralty, Samuel Pepys was to play no small part in the implementation of this policy which owed much to England's disastrous experiences at the hands of the Dutch navy in the early 1660s. Secondly, there was an increasing interest in woodland on the part of the large landowners, partly for economic reasons but almost equally for aesthetic ones which were bound up with what might be called the 'era of the landscape gardener'. Thirdly, but by no means least, it was the effect of the enclosure movement which brought in hedgerows to act as boundaries on a far greater scale than formerly. Incidentally, these hedgerows often had the result of preserving large numbers of individual trees as well as innumerable copses and spinneys which, given the exercise of the former rights of common, would otherwise soon have disappeared. Tucked away behind the hedgerow-palisades of individual landowners these small areas of woodland were relatively safe, at least from the sort of unorganized attack they had been under when forming a part of common land. It is thus to the enclosure movement that so many Midland shires owe their deceptively wooded appearance – without them few vestiges would now remain of Arden, Feckenham and Rockingham forests.

It was largely a combination of the Civil War and Sir John Wyntour of Lydney which threatened to bring the Forest of Dean into line with those of Arden and Rockingham. Arms were manufactured in the forest for the Parliamentarians and as late as July 1646 Colonel Birch, conducting the siege of Royalist Goodrich Castle writes that "we have supplies of shells for our grenadoes from the Forest of Dean". Gun Mills, near Flaxley Abbey, is said to be so named because cannon were manufactured there in the Civil War.

During the period of the Commonwealth it has been claimed that more than 40,000 trees were felled in the forest – though the government also made efforts to replant and to increase the afforested area. The government proposed to re-afforest 18,000 acres on the forest and this entailed the removal of four-hundred dwellings erected by illegal squatters. This seems to have led to what was very nearly a local uprising against the government. In May 1659 Colonel White reported to the House of Commons that:

> Upon the third day of this instant month divers rude people in tumultuous way, in the Forest of Dean, did break down the fences, and cut and carry away the gates of certain coppices enclosed for preservation of timber, turned in their cattle, and set divers places of the said forest on fire, to the great destruction of the young growing wood.

In 1662, consequent upon the Restoration of Charles II, Sir John Wyntour was restored to his rights and privileges in the forest. Samuel Pepys was responsible for drawing up the new document. A few months earlier, in February, had occurred the 'Great Gale' in the area of Dean and this too, found a mention in Pepy's Diary. "We have letters from the Forest of

Deane, that above 1,000 oakes and as many beeches are blowne down in one walke there".

The Great Gale was indeed a disaster. Large parts of the forest were left with scarcely a tree standing. Almost 26,000 oak trees were now fit for no more than charcoal and an additional 11,000 tons of fallen timber were earmarked for the Navy. Sir John Wyntour's hopes to fell even more of the forest timber were something that many local inhabitants now began view with apprehension. But the agreement went ahead and on the 20th June 1662 Samuel Pepys records:

> Up by 4 or 5 o'clock, and to the office, and there drew up the agreement between the King and Sir John Wyntour about the Forest of Deane; and having done it, he comes himself, whom I observed to be a man of fine parts: and we read it, and both liked it well. That done, I turned to the Forest of Deane, in Speede's Mapps, and there he shewed me how it lies; and the Lea bayley with the great charge of carrying it to Lydney, and many other things worth knowing.

Five months later, however, the Forest of Dean was to be discussed by some members of the newly formed Royal Society who were perhaps apprehensive about the felling operations which Wyntour had now begun. On the 5th November John Evelyn was to write that there was a meeting of the Society and "afterward meeting at Gresham's College, where was a discourse suggested by me concerning planting his Majesty's Forest of Dean with oake, now so much exhausted of ye choicest ship-timber in the world".

Complaints were now being made to the House of Commons about Wyntour's activities in the forest and a Commission was appointed to look into the situation. Shortly afterwards Sir John Harboard reported to the House "that Sir John Winter had 500 cutters of wood employed in Dean Forest, and that all the timber would be destroyed if care should not be speedily taken to prevent it".

This report was also accompanied by certain recommendations for the management of the Royal Forest – including a proposal that Sir John Wyntour should lose most of the rights he had been granted there – prepared by "the Freeholders, Inhabitants and Commoners, within the Forest of Dean". The proposals were later to form the basis of the Dean Forest Reafforestation Act of 1668, but as Parliament was now prorogued they were not immediately to be put into effect.

All this was a clear indication of the growing concern with English woodland for it was increasingly coming to be realized that the nation's timber resources – not only in Dean but equally in the New Forest and elsewhere – were dangerously close to exhaustion. All this placed Sir John Wyntour's felling operations for the dual needs of his ironworks and the Navy in jeopardy. In the spring of 1667 he had a number of meetings with Samuel Pepys and on 15th March Pepys records that, "This morning I was called up by Sir John Winter, poor man, come in a sedan from the other end of town, about helping the King in the business of bringing down his timber to the sea-side in the Forest of Dean".

In the Act of 1668 the licenses granted to Sir John Wyntour and others in the forest were, in fact, confirmed but subject to a number of general conditions which greatly limited their effect. This included the enclosure of 11,000 acres of forest land for replantation by the Crown in which there were to be no rights of pasturage, estovers or pannage and where trees were not to be felled until they had been viewed by two justices of the peace. A further 13,000 acres, which were not to be enclosed for replanting, were to be subject to the same conditions. Mining and quarrying were forbidden in enclosed areas and the number of deer in the forest was to be limited. Freeholders, however, had the right to do as they wished with their own land within the forest, the rights of the freeminers were confirmed and the Crown re-asserted its rights to lease stone-quarries and coal mines.

Undoubtedly in a further attempt to preserve the timber supply in Dean, the Crown also began to adopt the policy of closing down ironworks in the actual area of the Royal Forest – although, of course, it could not prevent the continuance of those which had grown up outside its boundaries. By 1680 this policy had been so thoroughly pursued that no ironworks survived in the actual area of the Royal Forest. In consequence there had been a serious decline in iron-ore mining. This decline, however, was to be more than offset by the increase in coal-mining which enjoyed official encouragement as still further preserving the timber supply from use as fuel. From this time coal-mining became the main preoccupation of the freeminers and iron-ore mining to slip increasingly into second place.

In 1692 the Crown appointed a commission to enquire into the state of the Forest. One of its tasks was to consider the effect on the forest of the unlikely event of the Crown deciding to restore the abandoned ironworks to production. The commissioners firmly reported that this "would utterly destroy the Forest, now being the finest nursery for a navy in the world". The Crown was now adopting a policy of felling almost exclusively for naval needs and the woodlands were being rigorously protected against encroachments. Numerous evictions of illegal squatters also took place at this period.

But the situation was not destined to last. Government preoccupation with timber resources was to wane under the impact of more immediate problems. The 'Glorious Revolution' of 1688 saw two of the keepers' lodges, York and Worcester Lodges, burnt to the ground as a local protest against James II and, although Crown policy seems to have been maintained along the lines of the Act of 1668 during the reign of Queen Anne, the years of the early Hanoverians saw the administration of the forest seriously deteriorate.

In 1763 John Pitt, the Surveyor General of Woods, reported, in respect of the Forest of Dean, that "great spoil had been committed, and great quantities of wood and timber, amounting in value to £3,255, cut by the order of Sir Edmund Thomas, the late Surveyor-General, without warrant". The situation in England's woodlands had come, over the previous fifty years, to resemble conditions as they had prevailed during late medieval times, forest officials allowing illegal felling and sale of timber in return for a share of the proceeds. Over the country as a whole it was estimated that timber resources had been reduced by two-thirds over the preceding forty years. A considerable amount of this must have been consumed by the charcoal burners.

Illegal felling in the forests was now to eclipse poaching as the traditional lawbreaking activity of the woodlands. John Pitt reported that "everything in his power has been done to put a stop to them, but that the offenders had become so desperate and daring as to bid defiance to his deputies, and render every attempt of his in a summary way totally ineffectual". He instanced a case when "not long before, a number of persons in disguise had openly cut down two large timber-trees at Yorkley, in Dean Forest, and wounded several keepers who attempted to oppose them".

The local inhabitants were now beginning to turn on the Crown officials, very possibly because many of these officials were known to be corrupt and making considerable profits from the illegal sale of forest timber. The forest people could not see why such men should have the right to prevent them from making profits of their own. The deputy-surveyor, Thomas Blunt, was being intimidated and reported that "having formerly pulled down and destroyed many cottages, fences and enclosures he had latterly been obliged to desist, fearing his life and property were endangered by the repeated threats and insults of the encroachers and their party".

One abuse which the official found particularly difficult to check was that whereby the freeminers – who were allowed to use such timber as they thought necessary for their mining operations – would fell far more timber than they actually required for their own work and would sell off the rest to be shipped to Bristol. Not that the keepers were all that keen to stamp out illegal felling anyway. One of their 'perks' was the top of any stolen tree they discovered and the timber thieves made it a practice to leave the sawn-off tops as the keepers' 'pay-off'. Having received their traditional reward there was thus not much more than a moral inducement for the keepers to hunt out the thieves.

Despite the efforts of Thomas Blunt there had been a great increase in the number of illegal squatters in the forest. Miles Hartland, one of the forest officials told the Dean Forest Commissioners in 1788 that:

> the greater number of the cottagers are from the neighbouring parishes; but there are also a great many from Wales, and from various parts of England, remote from the Forest. They are detrimental to the Forest by cutting wood for fuel, and for building huts, and making fences to the patches which they enclose from the Forest; by keeping pigs, sheep and co., in the Forest all the year, and by stealing timber.

Some efforts were made to improve the preservation of the forest, particularly in the implementation of a recommendation of the Commissioners that more than two-thousand squatters should be evicted from their cottages and the cottages themselves pulled down.

Even so conditions did not seem to have greatly improved in the forest by the turn of the century. The comments of Lord Nelson – who had more than a casual interest in ship-timbering – when staying near Ross in 1802 bear this out.

> Nothing in it can grow self-sown [said Nelson,] for the deer bark all the young trees. Vast droves of hogs are allowed to go into the woods in the autumn, and if any fortunate acorn escapes their reach, and takes root, then flocks of sheep are allowed to go into the Forest, and they bite off the tender shoot.

Nelson saw reasons why the Forest had fallen on hard times and suggested a possible remedy.

> The reason, [he declared,] why timber has of late years been so much reduced has been uniformly told me – that, from the pressure of the time, gentlemen . . . were obliged to sell (their timber) to raise temporary sums – say to pay off legacies. The owner cannot, however sorry he may feel to see the beauty of his place destroyed, and what would be treble the value to his children annihilated, help himself. It has struck me forcibly that if the Government could form a plan to purchase of such gentlemen the growing oak, it would be a national benefit, and a great and pleasing accommodation to such growers of oak as wish to sell.

It is rather strange to see the future victor of Trafalgar anticipating the present-day policy of the Forestry Commission management of private woodland.

It may have been the posthumous influence of the great admiral that was partly responsible for the Dean Forest (Timber) Act of 1808. This virtually reenacted the legislation of the past hundred and fifty years. However, unlike its precursors, it was to be put into effect immediately – after all England was in the middle of its war with Napoleon and wooden walls were uppermost in many minds. One of the first results of this latest piece of legislation was a refusal by the Surveyor-General of Crown lands to re-lease the mid-forest area of Whitemead Park to Lord Berkley on the ground that agriculturally it had been neglected and its buildings had been allowed to fall into disrepair. On the credit side, however, Whitemead Park was said to be bearing fine timber which the Surveyor considered should be encouraged and extended by further plantation.

It was not until now that large scale replanting in Dean really got under weigh and from this time may be said to date the beginnings of modern management of the forest. However, Dean had not yet assumed its present preoccupation with the cultivation of timber. For a further century and a half its story was to be a two-sided one. Now, at the beginning of the nineteenth century, the forest again blossomed as an industrial centre – but now as part of the new industrial revolution whose sinews were coal and the power of steam.

In 1809 two tramways – the predecessors of later railways – made their first appearance in the forest, largely to carry locally produced coal and timber. The Severn and Wye Valley Railway opened a line that ran from Lydney to Lydbrook while the Bullo Pill Company ran from Bullo Pill, on the Severn Estuary to Churchway. The Severn-and-Wye-Valley railway was later extended into some of the new plantation areas and the company also opened a line to serve the forest which ran from Monmouth. Steam engines also began to make their appearance, mainly for pumping water from the shafts and in this connection were to be introduced at Birches Well, the 'Catch Can' and Ivy Moorhead amongst a number of other pits. Engines were also set up at Vallet's Level, Howlett's Slade and Churchway Coal mines – with the result that these traditionally shallow Dean workings could now be operated at a far deeper level than formerly. Incidentally, most of the miners lived outside the actual boundary of the forest. As more workers became necessary the villages began to increase in size, Cinderford soon growing to the point where it justified its own corn mill. During the 1820s more collieries were opened up in the forest, including two at Park end. All were to be served by tramway connecting with the Bullo-Pill and Wye-Valley lines, which had been linked at Churchway Summit in 1823.

The new movements in the forest, both in industry and in forest management, were to lead to serious local disturbances.

Many ordinary foresters considered that they were being illegally deprived of their rights of common. The Forest of Dean riots of 1831 may have had some slight connection with the agricultural labourers' revolt of the previous year which, though it had been mostly confined to the eastern and south-eastern English counties, had also led to some isolated incidents in Gloucestershire.

The foresters found a leader in Warren James who seems to have sincerely believed that the foresters rights were being eroded. This local reaction was strongly supported by a virtual 'home-rule' newspaper, *The Forester*, published in Newnham. Edward Machen, the Deputy Surveyor, attempted to allay the foresters' fears and was later to record that:

> Warren Janes had for some time been urging others to join him in the recovery of their rights, which they considered to be usurped by foreigners, in whose hands the principal coal-works of the Forest are, by purchase or lease from the free-miners; and on the 3rd June he had a hand-bill printed, calling upon all persons to meet and clear the Forest on Wednesday June 8th. I spoke to him on the 5th, and told him in the presence of numbers the folly and danger of his proceedings; but he paid no attention, and said the Forest was given up to them in Parliament the year before; that he had a charter, which he would bring a show me. I published a notice, warning all persons not to join an unlawful assembly, and on Tuesday the 7th., Mr. Ducarel and I issued a warrant to apprehend him; but it could not be executed. We swore in a number of special constables, and with the woodsmen mustered about forty at the scene of action where they were to begin; but the rioters mustered nearly 200, with axes, and c., and began their work of destruction about 7 o'clock, and we found it useless to attempt to stop them. They were soon joined by othes, and supplied with cider, and continued their work, Wednesday, Thursday, Friday and Saturday, in which time they destroyed nearly one-third of the fences in the Forest, the reparation of which cost about £1,500.

Edward Machen considered that "nearly 2000" people were "involved in the work of devastation". Warren James was ultimately captured and sentenced to be transported for life. Later however, like Dorset's Tolpuddle Martyrs, he was to be pardoned, but never returned from Australia. In fact, once James reached Australia he seems to have disappeared from the face of the earth and he was never heard from again.

The riots of 1831, however, were only a temporary hiatus in the general progress of putting the Dean timber cultivation on an economic footing. Work was also proceeding in other directions, including the building of churches for the expanding population, the provision of schools – the latter including ones at Blakeney Hill, Ruardean Woodside and Viney – and of course, in house building. By 1854 it was possible for a government commission of inquiry into the Forest of Dean timberlands to report in glowing terms:

> Viewing these plantations as a whole we feel quite justified in representing to your Lordships (of the Treasury) that not only is their state such as to merit approval, but having reference to their regularity, growth, and prospective ultimate development, they are not surpassed by any Forest property in the kingdom.

Apart from the Dean iron manufacture the forest was now essentially the area that it has remained to the present day.

The re-introdution of iron manufacture in the forest had occurred in 1795 when a furnace was opened at Cinderford fired by coked coal. However it could not compete with the well established works of the North and Midlands. David Mushett's furnace at Whitecliffe near Coleford, which was opened in 1799, also failed to make headway and Mushett was to declare that iron manufacture could not hope to be revived in the forest. He was to be proved wrong by a local man Moses Teague who was to succeed, ironically using much of Mushet's equipment. Teague formed a company which:

> took a lease of Park End Furnace about the year 1825, erected a large water-wheel to blow the furnace, and to work in 1826. Mr Teague . . . formed the first 'Cinderford Iron Company' . . . The scheme comprehended two blast furnaces, a powerful blast engine . . . finery, forge, and rolling-mill, designed to furnish about forty tons of tinplate per week with collieries and mine work.

The Park End iron works also dates from the end of the eighteenth century, but like the Cinderford Iron Company, was not really a success until the mid 1820s. In 1827 "an immense water-wheel", was erected at Park End works, "51 feet in diameter and six feet wide, said to be nearly the largest in the kingdom". The company also "formed extensive and suitable ponds and canals for the supply of water. This water-wheel was but little used, in consequence of the general introduction and superior advantages of steam power, which was obtained by erecting an engine for creating the blast".

Tinplate manufacture forged ahead in Dean during these years with works being established at Park End, while the local Allaway family controlled works at both Lydney and Lydbrook. In later years the Lydney works came under the ownership of Richard Thomas – but, like many of the forest's former industrial centres, they are now closed.

Two blast furnaces operated at Soudley some five miles south of Cinderford in the middle years of the last century and iron had been mined in this area since at least the middle of the sixteenth century. In 1856 it was estimated that the Dean iron manufacturers were producing more than 24,000 tons of iron annually from the eight blast furnaces then working in the forest. It hardly needs to be said that, unlike the earlier industry, this later re-incarnation, being coal-based, scarcely offered a threat to home woodland. In this same year it was estimated that the Dean iron-ore mines were annually producing more than 100,000 tons of ore. Some mines were now quite deep and were equipped with heavy pumping engines, that at Soudley's Shakemantle Mine being capable of raising 198 gallons per stroke.

The Forest of Dean iron-industry prospered very largely because of the presence of relatively easily worked coal deposits. In contrast to the Wealden industry, that in Dean had not begun to decline faced with a combined shortage of both fuel and raw material but, as has already been mentioned, as a direct result of Crown policy which led to a closure of local ironworks. Once coal took over from charcoal as the primary fuel for the smelting process the way was open for the forest to re-emerge as an iron-manufacturing centre.

Such was hardly the case for the Weald. While the 1820s marked the renascence of the Dean iron industry they also marked the knell of that of the Southern counties. The iron industry had once covered much of the three counties of Surrey, Sussex and Kent, even straying across into Hampshire. At the opening of the nineteenth century it survived only in Sussex. There was still iron-ore to be found in the Weald, but it was becoming increasingly uneconomic to work it. Local timber resources had long ago given out and the cost of transporting coal was obviously not an expense faced by rival iron foundries in other parts of the country. It was the cost of coal transportation that was to push up the price of Wealden iron to the point where it could not longer compete with that from other centres. As long as the industry had remained wedded to charcoal the Weald had been in a dominating position. But once coal became the primary fuel of the iron industry the Weald was doomed.

With much of its raw material and fuel having to come from outside, the local iron industry managed to weather the first decade of the nineteenth century only because of the inflated demand for its products that was brought about as a result of the Napoleonic Wars. The fact that the Quaker ironmasters of Shropshire refused to manufacture cannon at this time must have been something welcomed by the remaining Wealden ironmasters. But in the post-war depression that followed Waterloo, the Sussex industry was to be one of the hardest hit and furnaces rapidly went out of production.

By the mid 1840s there were no ironworks functioning in the Weald. Wealden iron was a thing of the past. There was no longer smoke from the ironworks' chimneys and the slag heaps, which had once smouldderered almost continuously, became overgrown and very quickly forgotten. Before the century was out there was little more than a few place names to recall that this had once been an industrial area. Today there survives almost nothing to tell us that this was once the Black Country of the South.

The closure of the Wealden industry – and even the earlier introduction of coal-smelting – had come too late to save more than a mere fragment of the once widespread local woodland. As there had been no Crown forest land in the region at the time late seventeenth-century government came to take a serious interest in the nation's timber resources, the Weald had naturally been outside the scope of legislation designed to preserve and replant royal forest area. The Weald had been in private hands and most of its landowners had continued to sell off their timber to the ironworks without any policy of replanting. Lord Nelson's comments on the Forest of Dean would have been even more appropriate if they had been applied to the eighteenth-century history of Wealden timber. Only Ashdown and St Leonard's Forests survived, together with some small, scattered woodlands, into the mid nineteenth century. They still do and serve to give some indication of the Wealden landscape before the advent of the Sussex ironmasters.

Yet the Weald was far more fortunate than many other forest areas which, like the Forest of Morfe which once ran south from Bridgnorth to the Worcestershire border, had already been eaten away by the iron and other industries. Morfe seems have emerged relatively unscathed into the sixteenth century for, in 1540, Leland was to record that "Morfe is hilly ground, well wooded; a forest or chase, having deer". Perhaps the earlier wastage was not evident to Leland, but it must have been considerable for, two centuries later, the former forest had almost ceased to exist. This was a process which had undoubtably been accelerated by the Shropshire iron industry, which pre-dated the Darby connection with Coalbrookdale considerably. By the early eighteenth century Campden was writing of "Morfe, once a great forest adjoining Bridgnorth but now a waste with scarce a tree upon it". However, some fairly large areas of timber did survive in the former forest area though, when considered in connection with the former extent of the forest, they were hardly remarkable. The waste land was to disappear with the new enclosures, what remained coming to be called Morfe Common – although it was not a common in the strict sense of the term. The 'common' became the site of a local race meeting as the *Gentleman's Magazine* of 1764 records "there is a walk round Castle Hill (Bridgnorth) kept in good order, which commands a prospect of the low town, the river, and the common called Morfe, where the races are kept . . . There is also a pleasant walk on Morfe which affords a charming view of the adjacent country." In 1806 Morfe Common was itself enclosed and what remains of it is now a public recreation ground. The name survives as one of the Bridgnorth District electoral wards and less obviously in the name of Morville, a village some three to four miles north-west of the town. Few people would realize that the waterside recreation ground is the last remnant of a forest which was once indistinguishably linked to that of Kinver.

In the south the New Forest is the one great area of surviving woodland that stands largely outside at least one of the major preoccupations of this chapter. Fortunately for future generations its woodland was not generally associated with deposits of iron-ore as was the case in the Weald, Dean and South Staffordshire. An iron industry appeared here only in a small way and that limited to the southern tip of the forest. It closed down because of a shortage of local ore, and made little impact on the woodland. Apart from this the forest was largely Crown land. As such it was to be maintained and encouraged by Acts of Parliament very similar to those applied to the Forest of Dean. In fact, in the eighteenth century, even more than Dean, the New Forest came to be regarded almost solely as a nursery for naval timber. Lying on the South Coast, with traditional centres of shipbuilding close at hand, this was only natural.

The only time in post medieval years when the New Forest timber was to be seriously threatened on an organized scale was during the reigns of the early Stuarts. Both James I and Charles I found great difficulty in raising money through normal Parliamentary channels. When Charles, in 1629, decided to dispense with Parliament altogether and inaugurated the eleven years of personal rule – which the Parliamentarians were later to refer to as the 'Eleven Year Tyranny' – he was hard put to it to finance the royal Treasury. Amongst many other courses to which he resorted in these years was the selling of royal-forest timber under license. We have already met with the activities of Sir John Wyntour in the Forest of Dean and these were to be repeated by a motley collection of licensees in the New Forest. Although the timber resources of the area were naturally depleted as a result the very existence of the forest was never called into doubt in the way that of the Forest of Dean was to be by Wyntour's peculiarly cavalier treatment.

Nevertheless the depletion of New Forest timber resources gave rise to great government anxiety in the latter part of the seventeenth century. Again, as was the case with the Forest of Dean, this was largely because it was feared that England would soon cease to be self-sufficient in relation to the supply of naval timber. In 1688 an Act was passed for the "Increase and Preservation of Timber in the New Forest and in the County of Southampton". This obviously referred not only to the New Forest, but also to the Forest of Bere, the Alice Holt Forest, Woolmer Forest and the Forest of Avington (Parkhurst) on the Isle of Wight. Of these five forests that of Woolmer is no longer with us. It did survive into the present century, but in the later 1920s was taken over by the War Department as an extension to the Aldershot District training grounds. There had been plans to turn it into a largely conifer plantation. Recent legislation may once again make the area accessible to the public.

With the exception of Woolmer – which was largely a tract of healthland – all these southern forests had as their main function, from the late seventeenth to the mid-nineteenth centuries, the growing of oak for naval use. Except in the case of the New Forest, however, the Act of 1688 seems to have been a dead letter. In respect of the New Forest it was to be strengthened by another Act passed ten years later. By this the Crown was given the right to enclose up to 6000 acres, with the removal of common rights, for the planting of oaks for the navy. Two thousand acres were to be closed immediately and two hundred acres *per annum* thereafter. With occasional lapses this policy was generally followed for the next century and a half, at the end of which time about 10,000 acres had been planted, mainly with oak. The enclosed areas were thrown open for the use of the commoners as soon as it was considered the new growth was unlikely to be harmed by their animals.

Such a systematic policy can hardly be said to have been applied to the other Hampshire woodlands. The administration of these was nothing less than chaotic, especially in regard to the Alice Holt Forest and the Forest of Bere. Bere was administered by a non-resident Warden and a Court of Verderers with few actual powers while Alice Holt was leased to the Lieutenant of Woolmer, apparently as a form of pay, for the Lieutenant seems to have been able to do very much what he liked with the forest. As a result there was a great amount of felling and very little – if any – replanting. In 1811 the Lieutenant was relieved of his responsibilities and a year later an Act was passed authorizing the enclosure of 1,600 acres of Alice Holt, the local commoners being compensated for the loss of their traditional rights by land awards outside the re-defined area of the forest.

Despite the possession of a Warden and Court of Verderers, the position in the Forest of Bere was as bad, if not worse, than that at Alice Holt. Throughout the eighteenth century it was whittled down by numerous encroachments for agricultural use, by growing numbers of illegal squatters and by considerable indiscriminate felling – again with little attention being paid to replanting. In 1792 a Commission of Inquiry reported that the forest had shrunk to 16,000 acres much of which was in a very poor condition. In view of this it recommended the same sort of policy that was later to be adopted with the Alice Holt Forest, namely that the best areas of the forest should be enclosed and devoted to timber production the commoners being compensated for the loss of their rights by land grants made to them from the remainder. An Act carried these recommendations into effect in 1810. The position of Warden was abolished and in its place was put a Deputy Surveyor responsible to the Office of Crown Woodlands, and who also had responsibility for the forest land in the Isle of Wight. The Court of Verderers, whose rights and duties had been steadily contracting over the past 150 years, was to linger on until 1877. At the moment the Forest of Bere, which is now managed by the Forestry Commission, is under some threat in view of proposals to create a new urban conurbation based on Portsmouth.

The Isle of Wight Forest of Avington was generally considered to be another mainstay of the navy's timber supply – yet, in fact, it supplied very little of the Navy's needs. This was largely because, due in the main to poor management, so little of the timber produced was suitable. Here it was hardly the incursions of the commoners and their animals that was the trouble, for the forest undergrowth was so thick that, in places, it was almost impenetrable. It was this lack of thinning and clearing that made Avington such a loss during the eighteenth century. The thick undergrowth was growing at the expense of the trees. Even as late as the mid nineteenth century the estate manager was of the opinion that it could never produce good timber in any quantity. The poor state of Avington led one of the Commissioners of Woods, in 1849, to declare

> Let us hope . . . in future the interests of the Crown will be confined to experienced officers of known ability, educated in the management of woodland property and capable of directing whatever powers the Royal Forests may possess, to the great ends for which they are established – income and such timber as the purveyor of the navy can conscientiously accept for the dockyards.

In many ways this was not so much a criticism of the management of Avington – though that had been deplorable – but of many other areas of Royal Forest as well.

In the North the situation found at Avington came close to being repeated at the Forest of Delamere. Here the Crown officials short-sightedly planted oak which could hardly have been expected to flourish in the barren, sandy soil. The policy was not to be altered until the early 1850s when, with shipbuilding now making increasing use of iron, the Crown began to review the naval timber policy with its natural preoccupation with oak. Earlier, in 1812, Delamere Forest had been described as "sandy waste, virtually denuded of trees by the right holders". The forest had been continually shrinking and, at that time, was estimated to be about 8000 acres in extent. It was declared to enclose half this area which would be concentrated upon timber production and, as in the case of the southern forests, to compensate the commoners for the loss of their rights by dividing the remaining area between them.

So far, except in the case of the Forest of Morfe, we have dealt largely with the surving remnants of Royal-Forest land. Yet these were not the only woodland areas to be affected by the movements of the seventeenth and eighteenth centuries. Partly. due to enclosure, partly to industry, the Midland forests of Rockingham and Feckenham almost entirely disappeared. Yet remnants of former Royal Forest and private woodland did remain, especially in such Midland counties as Northamptonshire and Huntingdonshire. The ancient Royal Forest of Whittlewood was to survive as Hazelborough Forest – once merely one of the greater forest's walks – as too were Salcey Forest, Yardley Chase and other areas of woodland. The preservation of woodland in these regions can be accounted for by the same reasons that once called King William's Forest Laws into being. This was the heart of aristocratic hunting country and landowners could be expected to maintain large areas of woodland as cover for game. Foxhunting was to be responsible for the preservation of much woodland when areas of remaining scrub would be enclosed for coverts and nature left to do the rest. At least two of the Quorn's coverts – Thorpe Tussells and Ashby Pastures –originated in this way. In less wooded parts of the country many of the gorse clumps, whose burnished flowers seasonally enliven the more open countryside, came into being for much the same reasons – also, incidentally, to discourage nineteenth century fox-poachers from stealing the young cubs.

But many a Master of Foxhounds did not take kindly to that aspect of the enclosure movement which went some way towards at least giving the lowland countryside the appearance of being well-wooded. Hedgerows became necessary to divide one privately held holding from another and the older huntsmen favoured an open chase rather than one involving much jumping. In the early years of the nineteenth century R. S. Surtees, the creator of Mr Jorrocks, was to write

> there is little doubt that many of the large fields we still see, parts of common lands enclosed within the present century, will gradually become smaller and smaller as the land becomes richer and more valuable; until hunting will be a sort of hopping-in-and-out, clever sort of thing all day.

Surtees, like many of the hunting fraternity, linked hedgerows together with canals and railways as a threat to their sport. It was very largely the hedgerows that ended the open nature of much of the English countryside as it had existed for most of the previous three centuries. In many parts of England, especially in the Midland counties, the hedgerows were later, in alliance with those woodlands that still remained, to restore at least the illusion that England was a well wooded country.

The fox and shooting coverts, however, if they added to the area of wooded countryside were also the preserves of the game laws. Some were known to be so infested with man-traps, spring-traps and spring-guns that the hunts were at great pains to keep their packs away from them. Even the humble rabbit-poacher had to contend with the enmity of armed gamekeepers, for the rabbits were the gamekeepers' traditional perquisites and they were allowed to set traps for them. Not until the close of the 1830s did the private woodlands cease to be potentially lethal human slaughter-houses.

In the region of some Royal-Forest land, particularly in Hampshire, around the Forest of Dean and in the region of Delamere Forest, there still survived tracts of privately owned woodland. Some of this had been illegally gained in the past, some had survived the process of enclosure. In many cases much of this was to survive into the present century and now forms part of the forest areas administered by the Forestry Commission. But, by the end of the nineteenth century, a new threat had been created to the private woodlands in the form of the new system of death-duty taxation. In many cases woodland was to be sold off to meet the new tax and it was also to act as a serious deterrent to any policy of plantation in private woodland, for owners now became concerned for immediate returns rather than for planting what might or might not come to benefit their descendants.

Some extensive areas of private woodland did remain, notably in the West Midlands, in the forests of Wyre and Kinver, and in the scattered forest of Clun. Wyre had been seriously denuded by the activities of the charcoal burners and had shrunk to less than its present extent of 6000 acres. Kinver had, in many ways, been lucky to escape the devastation that the south Staffordshire iron-industry had wrought in nearby Cannock Chase, large areas of which had been reduced to scrub and heathland. In Clun and the slightly more southerly forest of Mortimer – both of which had once been continuous with the Forest of Morfe – woodland survided largely on the poorer hillside soils, the lowlands having been enclosed for agriculture and the remainder of the hills being devoted to sheep grazing.

In the West some woodland did remain in what was known as the Royal Forest of Dartmoor, though it is doubtful if much of the Dartmoor area was ever really true forest – at least in historical times – and the term would seem to have implied that Dartmoor, like Exmoor, was not a woodland forest but a royal hunting chase.

Already mentioned is that fact that the landscaping activities of many more wealthy landowners greatly helped to foster the illusion that England was more wooded than it really was. Thus at Woodstock there was to be the landscaping of Blenheim Palace which, incidentally helped to preserve what remained of the Forest of Wychwood. At Croombe Court, which Capability Brown was to landscape for the Earl of Coventry, this doyen of the art of landscape gardening was painstakingly to create a wooded parkland upon land which had hitherto been considered unreclaimable heath and bog. This practice of emparking large areas of landed estates, partly for aesthetic and ornamental purposes, partly for the keeping of deer and partly to ensure an adequate local timber supply was responsible for the retention of much remaining woodland and for the plantation of some areas which had previously not been known to bear timber at all. Such places as the Earl of Bradford's estate at Weston-under-Lizard in Staffordshire, that of Lord Berwick at Attingham Park in Shropshire and especially the knot of landed estates in Nottinghamshire long known as 'The Dukeries', all emparked various areas of woodland and they and others like them, helped to prevent the complete deafforestation of former forest land.

In other areas tracts of woodland were to survive partly because they were relatively inaccessible and partly because they were on poor agricultural land which did not justify the cost of their removal. To causes such as these are due the survival of the hangers of the south, the denes of the north-east and the hardwood woodlands that cover many steep valleys. Near Canterbury the Blean Woods were to survive because the clay soil was too difficult to work – and the same was to be true for Surrey's Ashtead Woods. Woodland was also planted to restore protective cover to arable fields and in some cases just for the pleasure of creating a conspicuous landmark, as in the case of Wittenham Clumps which overlook the Thames below Oxford.

However, the reclamation of some forest areas was not all in favour of reafforestation. Reafforestation was a policy to be pursued with vigour on the Crown woodlands, but disafforested land in private hands only occasionally went the same way. In the Cannock-Chase region the denudation of much of the chase for the needs of the South Staffordshire iron-industry during the fifteenth and later centuries had left a land which very soon developed into a bog. In a naturally ill-drained area the tree cover had earlier been the main agent in keeping the land from becoming water-logged. Once the cover was removed the land quickly became an unusable waste.

However, in this particular case, large bog-ridden areas were to be reclaimed due to the interest of one of the largest local landowners, Edward Littleton of Teddesley Hall. Littleton succeeded to his estate in 1812 and was destined, by necessity, to become something of an expert in the problems of agricultural drainage. Much of the machinery used in the work was his own invention. It was inevitably a slow process, but over a period of twenty-five years, he increased the acreage of his agricultural land by almost four thousand acres and was to boast that his rickyards were the largest in England.

In many respects Cannock has close resemblances to Dean, especially in the fact that both iron-ore and coal were mined in both localities. The small-scale mines of the chase have long ceased working and coal-mining is now limited to a few large pits. With the present re-emphasis on coal as a major national fuel however, the number of pits in the area may reasonably be expected to increase.

One colliery enterprise of the last century – at Norton Canes – was associated with the father of Jerome K. Jerome, the author of the classic *Three Men in a Boat*. The Rev. Jerome Clapp Jerome came to South Staffordshire from Appledore in

1855 to undertake work for the Walsall Congregationalists. Preaching, however, was hardly likely to make him a fortune and he hoped to invest money which had come to his wife Margueritte in profitable coal-working. When the Rev. Jerome put his money into the Conduit Colliery at Norton Canes it had a good prospect of success. It was known that there was coal to be found in the region and he had experienced men to help him. But, like many men before him, Jerome was to be bedevilled by geology. Water and running sand proved too difficult for him to combat. He ran out of capital and the mine was flooded. In later years Jerome's Conduit Colliery workings were taken over by the Holcroft family who succeeded in workings on the Cannock coalfield. However, it was now more generally known as Jerome's Pit – so the preacher from Devon had at least made his mark on his adopted heath.

With a few exceptions the general conditions and extent of English woodland as it exists today had been established by the 1850s. In some places, such as Woolmer, more forest land was destined to be lost in the future. But in the surviving forest areas – especially in the Crown woodlands – the actual extent of the woodlands was destined to increase.

The planting of conifer softwoods was already beginning to make a mark on the old hardwood woodlands – though Delamere Forest was the only English forest which historically had been primarily devoted to conifer production. However, as the need for naval oakwood declined in the second half of the nineteenth century it became possible to introduce conifers as an economic crop, at least on land which favoured them more than the traditional oak. It is, of course, the spread of the conifer plantation, which has most altered the character of English woodland over the last century. However, even allowing for this and for some growth in the actual extent of English woodland over the past one hundred years, the basic pattern and area of English woodland has remained much the same since the mid nineteenth century. Today it is not so much movements in forestry, but in agriculture in general, that threaten to alter the landscape of the English countryside.

7

Chippings and Cinders: Forest Remains

Most of England ceased to be forest more than four centuries ago. Yet today, even in areas where there is no longer anything but the most scattered vestige of woodland, there exist survivals of what could be called the age of timber. Most obviously these survivals are in the form of the few industries which originated in connection with the forest and in our heritage of half-timbered buildings. Less obviously the former woodlands are still echoed through many place-names and surnames.

Early surnames fell largely into two broad categories, those derived from place and those derived from occupation. The most general of forest place-names which also became a major form of surname is that of ley, a ley being originally a man-made clearing in the forest. Thus we have a number of surviving forms of this as Leigh, Lea, Lee existing as surnames in their own right and a very large number of surnames which include it as a suffix as in Bradley, Hadley, Burley and so forth. In the case of the latter the name will often have come from an association with settlements which grew up in the clearings and their origin tends to be somewhat later than those which use the 'ley' form on its own. There are a number of compounds such as Leighton which fuse place with occupational origins. The forest regions themselves gave rise to a considerable number of surnames of which the various forms of Dean would appear to be the most common, perhaps reinforced by the fact that a 'dene' was often the description for a particular area of woodland.

The occupational derivations of such surnames as, for

example, Miller, Smith and Carter are obvious. But time has partly obscured the origin of many others. Especially in the Forest of Dean the surnames Coles, Cole and Colley were, and in some areas still are, particularly common. These originated in connection with the charcoal-burning industry and, like many other surnames, long outlived the source of their inspiration. One of the most vague surname survivals is that of Ward – implying the office of warden – and which could originate from any of a host of minor hereditary posts involving the guardianship of some aspect of royal, and occasionally private property. Some other 'ward' survivals are more specific such as Woodward, or 'wood guard', and Hayward, a 'hay' being an area of enclosed woodland. The surname Wood is sometimes a corruption of 'ward', sometimes a contraction for the various prefixes which meant 'of the wood' and of which Attwood is one. Other forest surname survivals include Bowyer, a maker of bows, Sawyer, a timber miller, Turner, a woodworker and Fletcher, a maker of arrows.

A few names may at first glance seem timber-based but are not, including Walker, which does not generally originate from a forest walk but from the trampling process that went on in early fulling mills, and Catchpole which had nothing to do with felling or inspecting trees but was the name given to some local law officers. A few names are of indeterminate origin but may be connected with the forest. One is that of Field for an Anglo Saxon 'feld' was often a clearing made on the edge of forest land. There are a large number of names taking trees as their origin such as Oak, Ashe and Rowntree and the names Forest and Forester speak more clearly of their origins than any others.

Traditional forest industries survive in a few areas. Charcoal burning kilns still make occasional appearances in the New Forest, though these have a rather technological appearance and would scarcely be recognised by the charcoal burners of three centuries ago. There are no charcoal burners surviving in the Forest of Dean but a charcoal factory has now arrived to make up the deficiency.

Furniture making has long survived in Buckinghamshire in the area based upon High Wycombe, nowadays located there not so much because of proximity to the predominantly beech woodlands of the Childrens but because of a tradition of experienced craftsmanship. Although much of the modern industry is mechanized almost to the point of automation there is still a demand for the work of the skilled cabinet-maker, although the Buckinghamshire industry has always been basically concerned with the production of chairs of which the traditional Windsor chair is the most well known.

In many areas woodworking of a less sophisticated character has been revived to renew the tradition of the local carpenter. It may be a little sad to realize that the local blacksmith's shop, if there is one, is more likely to be engaged in the production of wrought iron gates and house name-plates than in shoeing horses or mending cart-wheels and that the local carpenter will probably be producing wooden trinkets such as spice-racks and fruit bowls. Yet, in general, the call for traditional craftsmanship at local level is small. In the past the work of local craftsmen, carpenters, thatchers, wooden clog-makers and blacksmiths was essential for the survival of the rural community. Modern communications and industrial techniques have put an end to this situation. In all but a very few cases the traditional craftsman is no longer a necessity. In our automated, mass-production age his products have largely become luxury items.

Basket-making, at least in its traditional form, is still linked to the woodland. There are now only three major centres of the craft – these being that of the Somerset Sedgemoor region which produces willow baskets, that of the Wyre Forest producing the oak spale basket and that of Sussex producing the trug basket and based upon the village of Hurstmonceaux.

In some areas boat-building still survives, but its dependence on wood is now minimal, for most of the leisure-trade craft are now combinations of metal and glass-fibre. However, there is still a demand for the largely wooden vessel and the trade of the traditional boat builder has enjoyed something of a revival in recent years.

One industry which has moved increasingly toward a reliance on timber over the past century is that of paper-making. Before 1870 paper was generally produced from discarded and sorted rags which were pounded to pulp as part of the paper-making process. With the increasing use of wood pulp from the end of the nineteenth century onward the paper-making industry has been moving some of its mills into forest areas to benefit from the low transportation costs of being near to the source of its raw material supply.

Yet if we are to ask what truly remains of the actual forests of our past we can only answer that they are with us in the structure of so many of our older buildings. The oak timbers that went to make the 'wooden walls' of England's Navy – it has been estimated that in the region of 2000 oak trees were required for one man-of-war – have rotted into oblivion. It cannot be claimed that our heritage of timber-framed buildings has fared all that well. Menaced by woodworm, rising-damp and man's incessant demand for modernity timber-framed buildings have collapsed, been masked and have been demolished all over the country. But in a society as frenetic as our own has been over the past two centuries, it is remarkable just how much has managed to survive.

In hilly, non-woodland areas such as the Cotswolds or the Peak District, the local domestic architecture is, as would be expected, largely of local stone. In former woodland regions the older examples are largely half-timbered, and there are still survivals of half timbered cottages in-filled with daub and wattle rather than with masonry. A very large proportion of the less important domestic architecture has disappeared and most survivers tend to be the more substantial examples. Only in such rare cases as Herefordshire's Pembridge is it now possible to find a complete village street of half-timbered buildings constructed on the small scale.

Of course, some small-scale medieval buildings do survive in the forest areas – but it has been the present century which has been responsible for the removal of so many, often for the sound reason that they had become unsafe and unhealthy. But, certainly in the forest regions, the periodic clearings of illegal squatters meant that few of the poorer dwellings could survive whilst in the agricultural countryside, the effects of the enclosure movements included the abandonment of many peasant homesteads. Of those that do remain many have been changed almost out of recognition by their new owners and it is certain that their original occupants would find it very difficult to believe that their once humble dwellings can now command many thousands of pounds on the property market.

Anglo-Saxon building was largely of timber and even the Romans mainly built in wood, reserving stone and brick for civic and more important domestic architecture. In the Middle Ages it was the Anglo-Saxon cruck construction that was to predominate in the English countryside. The war-lords might build their castles and keeps of stone – they had need to – but the successors of the land-based Anglo-Saxon nobility, the numerous manorial lords who formed the focal points of English rural life, lived with an architectural tradition that the alien nobility little altered. In the forests themselves even that hallmark of Norman influence, the stone built church, was often absent. Here churches, as well as manor houses, were half-timbered, even if the Normans were to give some a longer lifespan by placing them on stone piers.

Towns also were basically of timber, all of which had to come from the forests. Both town and country dwellings were largely roofed with thatch, a combination which immediately explains the complete and often repeated, burning out of many a medieval town. The Great Fire of London may have been the last great urban conflagration to be caused by accident – but there was scarcely a town in England that had not been burnt to the ground at least once during the Middle Ages. Worcester and Nottingham were both burnt out twice within the space of three years during the anarchic civil war of Stephen's reign.

It is surprising how durable some seemingly insubstantial rural buildings have proved. But this was not due so much to the quality of the materials used as to the nature of the ground on which they were sited. A dry, well drained site was obviously far preferable in the case of half-timbered, daub-and-wattle buildings than a damp, ill drained one. The houses of the rural poor were little more than huts, with earthen floors and support posts sunk straight into the ground without anything but the most rudimentary form of foundation. Often ill-roofed and windowless – glass remained a luxury item until the eighteenth century – if they did not have to be abandoned because of disease and filth, then they could hardly be expected to last more than a generation before they collapsed due to rotting timberwork. The stinking, insanitary hovels of the medieval poor, and of their successors into the seventeenth and eighteenth centuries, could not have been expected to survive into our own day.

What does survive from those times is building on a far less primitive scale – and which certainly was never occupied by the lowly agricultural workers and rarely by their peasant-proprietor descendants. Although many a renovated and modernized rural cottage would appear to befit the romantic conception of besmocked yokel seated contentedly alongside a plump and well fed wife and healthy, happy children with cider-jar and pipe to hand, it is doubtful if they ever took part in this 'artists's impression' of rural bliss. The yokel would have inhabited one of the rickety hovels, his wife would almost certainly have been spare rather than plump for her working life was at least as arduous as his own, and his children, far from being happy, would have been menial drudges probably suffering from rickets and with no more than a fifty-fity chance of living through a childhood of cold and sodden winters in an insanitary house crawling with disease.

The quaint cottages which do survive were very largely the homes of the rural wealthy, the homes of the prosperous yeoman-farmers who emerged during the three centuries following the Reformation. Their houses were less than the manor house itself but they were almost as important, for their appearance heralded a new commercialism in agriculture. They were not ostentatious if only because they were usually built by the yeoman and his family for whom practical considerations were foremost, and their derivation was to be that of the traditional agricultural hovel. Yet they were built soundly, their timber-frames placed upon stone foundations, and with timber used to strengthen as well as to support. It was in their roofing that they owed most to the past.

Apart from the building trade the major industries which still retain their connections with the woodland are now only four in number. These are basket-making, the furniture trade, tanning and boat-building at least two of which are under threat from both foreign competition and the increasing use of synthetic materials.

Basket making survives in the region of the Forest of Wyre

and in the former forest area of the Sussex Weald. There is also a considerable basket-making industry in Somerset but, as this lies beyond the bounds of the forest areas, it can only be relevantly considered in comparison with the two other centres.

The baskets made in Wyre are known as spale baskets and are made of interwoven oak laths or spales cut from coppice-grown oak. The baskets are round or oval in shape and their main advantage over the osier baskets of the West is that the weave is so close that even powdery materials can be carried in them. There is still a considerable industrial use for the spale basket which can carry anything from shellfish to cotton waste. The industry also survives in the once forest area of the Lancashire Furness peninsula.

A spale basket-maker begins making his basket by shaping the bool or rim. Usually made of hazel, this can also be of ash or oak. The rod is softened in boiling water until pliable and then bent to an oval shape, the two loose ends being fastened together with a nail. The oak from which the laths are made comes from the straight-growing rods to be found around the stumps of specially felled trees. The oak must be free of knots, straight grained and usually not more than thirty years old. The rods are cut into lengths between four and six feet long and, with their bark removed, are then boiled for many hours until they have become quite soft. Removed from the boiling vat a pole is then quartered by the craftsman using a beetle and wedge – a small wooden mallet and a splitting tool – and each quarter is then cleaved into thin strips between one and three inches wide. This is a skilful operation as the laths have to be the same thickness throughout their length.

Before the weaving process can begin the laths have to be smoothed and trimmed off with a fine spokeshave, for this is a job that cannot be undertaken after the completion of the basket. The finished laths are now placed in water and the stoutest will be used to form the warp of the basket. The basket-maker works from the centre outward, beginning with the longest lath and adding progressively shorter ones until either end is reached. The thinner, more easily worked laths are known as chissies and are now woven through the warp and around the bool until the whole basket is completed. The basket is now left to dry and the end product will be a highly durable basket of very considerable strength.

The trug-basket is the southern equivalent of the spale-basket. The frame is made of ash or chestnut the rods of which are first cut into a convenient length and cleft in two. The outer surface retains its bark while the inner is shaved and smoothed with a drew-knife and spokeshave. When each rod has been reduced to a width of two inches and is less than an inch in thickness it is steamed in an elm steaming-chest and when fully pliant is placed in an oval frame known as a setting brake. The overlapping ends of the frame rods are then nailed together. Pollard willow is used for the body of the trug. A pole is cleft to form strips of no more than $\frac{1}{8}$ in thick which are then smoothed into a crescent shape. The boards are steamed and their boatlike appearance is obtained by levering each between two wooden bars. An average trug-basket will contain seven boards, a centre board, two seconds at each side of this, followed by a pair of side boards for either side.

The trug is now assembled, using the boards which have been previously dipped in water to make them more pliable. Like the spale basket the trug is assembled from the centre outward, the centre board going in first, followed by the seconds and then by the side-boards. Each one is nailed to the frame by two nails at the centre and two at each end. The boards of a trug-basket overlap and appear rather like a diminutive version of a clinker-built boat. The basket is finally given stability by the addition of willow cross-pieces.

The three types of basket – osier, spale and trug – are all facing increasing competition from overseas and also from such bodies as the Blind Institution. However, the foreign baskets are very largely of the ornamental variety and if they offer a serious threat to some of the traditional wares of the osier weavers they have yet to make serious inroads into the market of the spale and trug makers.

Tanning is an industry which has long been associated with forest land or, to be more exact, with oaklands. Most early tanneries were situated near to the oak woods because the oak-bark, rich in tannin, was essential to the tanning process. Today oak-bark is still used in the process, though other elements are also made use of. A few tanneries still work exclusively with oak-bark, a considerable amount of which comes from the Forest of Dean.

The oak-bark was required for the process known as leaching. This involved placing the hides in vats containing progressively stronger solutions of tanning liquour until the whole hide was impregnated prior to its being dried and curried before it finally emerged as leather. Oak-bark was, in the past, largely obtained from coppiced-oak plantations, but is now more usually taken as a by-product of oak felled during the winter or spring. It is far easier to remove the bark from oak felled during the spring. The bark is removed by cutting around the tree at intervals of approximately two feet and then cutting vertical slits. In this way large semi-circular lengths of bark are obtained which are then stacked so that rain cannot penetrate them for the tannic is soluble in water.

Each tannery was equipped with a bark-mill where the bark was ground down to a fine powder. The ground bark was then taken from the mill and the tanning liquor was made in the leeching pits by adding cold water. The mixture was allowed to stand for some weeks before it was used. Like all traditional industrial techniques tanning has been affected by modern developments. Yet here the greatest changes have not been in the tanning methods themselves but in the rise of other industries in competition with traditional leather and which have tended to create a declining demand for leather products. The use of rubber and synthetic fibres has made inroads into the leather industry, though it must be said that unless these had been developed it would have found it impossible to keep pace with the demand for products, which until the advent of the age of the synthetic, had been the preserve of the leatherworker. The tannery at Colyton, Devon still tans its leather by the traditional process.

High Wycombe is now the centre of the English furniture industry yet, traditionally it was the centre of only part of this, namely chair-making. The making of a chair by traditional methods is divided up into six processes each of which is undertaken individually. Factory processes have tended to make the industry increasingly mechanized, but it is still possible to find craftsmen working in traditional fashion.

Each craftsman engaged in a particular part of the chair-making process has his own description. Thus it is the bodger who is responsible for cutting and shaping the basis of a beech chair-leg, the benchman who cuts the sawn parts of the chair, the bottomer who adzes the chair seat, the bender who makes the bow framing the back of the chair, the framer who smoothes the component parts of the chair, then assembles them using a wide variety of tools for shaping and boring and finally adds the stain. The last in line is the finisher and polisher though nowadays most of the processes used involve modern equipment such as spray guns.

The traditional bodger sets up his workshed in a beech glade. Having bought a stand of timber be selects those trees most suitable for his purpose and these must be neither too old nor too young. In the past the bodger's shed was made from nearby saplings, which formed a framework which was later walled with shavings and roofed over with thatch. But, in recent times, the shed has tended to be a prefrabicated one.

The felled trees are first sawn into billets and these are then cleft to produce pieces suitable for chair-legs. The pieces are then trimmed to a roughly octagonal shape and then shaved to very nearly the correct shape of the finished leg. Then follows the turning process using the oldest form of lathe still working – the pole lathe. The wood is still in the green and, after the turning process is complete, the finished legs are stacked to dry out before being taken to the Wycombe factories.

The bodger is the only one of the chair-making craftsmen who carried on his trade essentially in the open. All the others are now largely factory-based, although there are a few specialized craftsmen carrying on the trade in their own workshops. Perhaps the most skilled – certainly the one requiring the greatest number of skills – is the framer. The framer has to smooth the parts that come to him in a rough condition from the other workers. He had to tenon the various parts and to bore dozens of holes in legs, stretchers, bows and seats. The boring is a very skilled operation for the various stretchers and rails enter other parts of the chair at different angles. No patterns or written calculations are used for the boring, all of which is judged by hand and eye alone. The framer next has to assemble the chair which is then ready

An impression of Dick Turpin's ride to York. This one legendary event has clouded the real brutality of Turpin's short-lived career

Robin Hood, as a romantic nineteenth-century artist may have wished to imagine him

The Rufus Stone: the stone is said to mark the spot where William II (William Rufus) was killed by an arrow near Cadnam in the New Forest. There has been much speculation as to whether he was murdered or died by accident

A notable example of half timbered architecture: Queen Elizabeth's hunting lodge at Chingford, Essex

Charcoal burning: littering the stack prior to burning

The stages of preparation: (*right to left*) a stack half covered with litter, a stack fully covered and ready for firing, and two stacks almost burnt out. The awnings are erected for protection from wind and rain as the fire must be closely controlled

The tanner: a sixteenth-century woodcut showing the hide being prepared

A smelting house in Middleton Dale, Derbyshire. It was the discovery of coal smelting processes that largely saved England's forests from extinction

Abandoned ironstone workings. Known to have been worked in the sixteenth century these reputedly date from Roman times: the Scowles, near Lydney in the Forest of Dean

Horses are still used for haulage in the forest and can prove more economical than the use of tractors. Mr James Scott can pull out up to 1,000 cu. ft. in a week

Plaiting a hurdle. Although hurdle-making is not so widespread as formerly it is still a thriving rural craft

The trug-basket maker at work (Sussex)

Binding a besom

Walking-stick manufacture: polishing the handle

either for marketing in 'the white' or to be sent to the polishing shop.

The craft of the shipwright has altered greatly over the past century and a half. No one makes 'wooden walls' any more and iron and steel have taken over from oak for the construction of all larger vessels. Even for the building of smaller craft, oak has largely been edged out in favour of elm, wych-elm and even mahogany. Traditional methods have also been greatly affected by the increasing use of fibre-glass and moulded plastic, though a few boat-builting yards still uphold the older methods of production. Yet boat-building still uses a considerable amount of English timber, and has a history dating back to man's first dug-out canoe. A century and a half ago boat-building was almost entirely a manual craft, with no machinery being used other than a grindstone. Today most boat-yards are a nest of machinery with the power-saw having pride of place.

The first stage in the production of a boat is the cutting of patterns, either first chalked out on a loft-floor or incised on a soft-wood board known as a 'scieve board'. The patterns are then duplicated from thin strips of wood and, as a boatyard tends to turn out many boats from one pattern, the walls of the workshop are often hung with many patterns ready for use.

Yet, before the planks and timbers are assembled, the framework of moulded timbers, including keel, stem, and sternpost, must be prepared. Work begins with the keel and the attaching of the stem and stern-posts, followed by the floor timbers and keelson and then the futtocks, the curved timbers forming the side of the boat. The framework, which is considerably strengthened in those parts expected to take most strain, is then braced and held together by cross-timbers.

The boat has then to be planked, the first two planks being the most difficult to lay as there can be many curves and twists and the planks have to be rivetted to both the keel and to either end. The second plank has to overlap the first and be rivetted to this and to both ends. This process is followed up each side of the boat, with each plank being at a slightly different angle than that above or below it and yet at the same time having to fit perfectly otherwise the boat will let water. The moulded cross-struts are now put into place along the length of the boat. First held by copper nails they will be ultimately rivetted into place. A clinkerbuilt boat will not need to be caulked and a coat of lead paint will make it watertight. Carvel-built boats however, have side-planks meeting edge to edge and for them caulking is an essential. After caulking a boat is almost complete and the boat-builder now adds the three stringers, 'gunwale', 'rising' and 'bilge' which are attached all around the inside of the boat to impart added strength.

The examples quoted here have been of some of the more obvious trades in which the woodworking craftsman still survives as a recognisably traditional worker. Some, such as the spale and trug-basket makers may appear rather inconsequential, if not complete anachronistic in an age that prides itself on its technology rather than its basic techniques. But the woodworker was once the lynchpin of local society and a man who could not turn his hand to at least some element of the craft was at a tremendous disadvantage compared to the rest of his fellows. Our surviving craftsmen in wood may nowadays be viewed as piecemeal remnants of a rough-hewn age. But they survive still to stand alongside their tools and their material. At a time when the bowels of our earth are quivering in exhaustion after two centuries of thoughtless exploitation that have made the Age of Metal it may well be that we have need of the skills of these descendants of the men who once carved their names into an earlier Age of Wood.

The tools of the traditional wood-worker nowadays often enjoy a leading place in any museum's collection of craft industry relics. But no collection will be found to be identical. This is because the craftsman very often made a large number of his own tools whilst adapting others so that they more closely fitted his requirements. It was this, plus his own skill, that invested the craftsman's work with so much of its individuality – something which no amount of sophisticated, powered machinery can duplicate.

The other major element contributing towards the individualism of the craftsman's products lay in his choice of the materials for the job. Nowadays we are so accustomed to the use of timber-substitutes, plastics, fibre-glass, laminates, hardboards and so on, that most people could be forgiven for not knowing what type of wood was best for a particular purpose. But the traditional woodworker, whether in furniture making, shipbuilding, house building or general carpentry had to think in terms of the best. This was not an altruistic gesture on his part, but a sound business consideration. If his work did not give satisfaction he would very quickly find himself with no work to do. Those who employed his labours knew what they wanted. Even the man scratching a living by cutting clothes pegs had to cut good clothes pegs. Shoddy goods might be bought once – but not again. When mass-production came into being it was possible to flood traditional markets with shoddy goods at a price far less than that at which the craftsman could offer his own. Quality became an expensive commodity. It has remained so ever since.

Almost all types of English grown timber originally had their uses. It is well-known that oak was cultivated for ship-building, beech for furniture making and so on. It may not be so well-known that the timber of the rowan tree was once preferred for the making of cross-bows whilst that of the yew was most commonly used for the long-bow. Even the flimsy timber of the elder was once used by many cottagers as the piping for domestic forge bellows. Small boys preserve something of this use by using the smaller twigs for pea-shooters.

One English tree is thought to have derived its very name from one of the uses to which its timber was traditionally put. This is the hornbeam. Its timber is extremely hard and was once used to make the yokes for plough-drawing oxen. A beam of wood was attached to the horns of the oxen and the name may have derived from this. But it the timber of the hornbeam had this amongst many other agricultural uses it was also a prime timber for the charcoal burners. This was because it burnt very slowly at the same time giving off a very hot flame. In iron-smelting areas hornbeams were felled to the point of local extinction.

Native English timber still has a large number of individual uses, some of which appear rather esoteric. The timber of the white willow is used in the making of cricket-bats because it is both tough and relatively elastic. The saplings of another member of the willow family – the osier willow – provide the basic raw material for basket-making and for lobster-pots. Also in the small-timber category is the birch, which still provides punishment canes and, on a far smaller scale than formerly, the material for the manufacture of bessoms.

The timber of the aspen – a member of the poplar family *salicaceae* – is nowadays used chiefly for the manufacture of chip-baskets, matches and match-boxes. In the early days of aviation the ash provided the timber framework of aeroplanes and it is still sometimes used in the construction of some gliders. The resilience of this timber under stress accounts for its continuing use for such items as oars and hammer handles. Like the hazel it is also used in the surviving rural craft of hurdle-making, though in Kent the hazel is also cultivated for its nuts, the traditional Kent Cobs.

Of course, many of our trees are imports. The mulberry, for example, is nowadays to be found being largely planted in parks. But it was originally introduced in the seventeenth century when there were plans to encourage an English silk industry. The silk worms both lived and bred in the leaves of the mulberry tree. But by far the most evident imports to English woodlands have been in the form of conifers. The timber for the manufacture of most lead pencils comes from the American Red Cedar whilst the spruce provides the raw material for telegraph poles and railway sleepers as well as being the major timber used in the production of paper. The cone-bearing but deciduous larch is at present widely cultivated and much of its timber used in garden fencing and conifer timber in general meets many of the demands of the domestic building industry.

The present trend in many woodlands, both those managed by the Forestry Commission and those in private hands, such as those cultivated by Mr Noel Good of Culmington, near Craven Arms, on Wenlock edge is towards diversifying the number of species of timber growing on a given area of woodland as much as possible.

Thus it is possible to find larch, aspen, beech and spruce growing in close proximity to each other in some areas of cultivated woodland. The major obstacle to the general implementation of this form of woodland planting remains the long-term nature of most timber cultivation, good beech for example taking in the region of forty to sixty years to mature. It has been the private timber growers' need to obtain a quick return on his investment that has led to so much conifier planting taking place on private land. The situation is changing slowly, but it may well be four or five decades before the conifer ceases to dominate most of our woodland areas.

Of course, the crafts we have considered here are not the only ones surviving in England which use the products of the forest. Related to the basket-maker is the hurdle-maker, whose trade is enjoying a fitful revival at the moment, and at the risk of being esoteric, there has even been a revival in such trades as that of the wooden clog maker whose wares, in the past, were not confined in use to the milltowns of the North and Midlands but were used by agricultural workers all over the countryside.

But the trades mentioned in this chapter are the major working survivors of our woodland industries. They still produce essential products rather than ornamental or luxury ones. Nonetheless, they are only the remnants of an economy and a way of life which was essentially tied to the timbered countryside – and even they are threatened. The great age of timber is passed. Perhaps the efforts of a few craftsmen will ensure that it never completely ends.

8

Forests Without Trees

Considering that not so long ago, most of lowland England was once forest land, it is rather surprising to find that the description 'forest' has been retained for only a few areas of once-wooded land. England's major forests-in-name-only are four in number, two lying in the southwest, namely the Forests of Exmoor and Dartmoor, one, the Forest of Arden lying in the Midlands and the other, the Forest of Bowland being in the North.

Strictly speaking it is seriously doubted in some quarters, if some of these areas were ever forests at all. Particularly in the case of the Royal Forest of Dartmoor it would appear that the medieval description of this as a forest merely implied that the 'great waste' came under the laws of the forest in terms of administration because it was a royal hunting ground. In general this is certainly true, though parts of Dartmoor were doubtless wooded in medieval times and timber land is at the present day maintained there both by the Forestry Commission and by private landowners. Nevertheless, even today woodland forms only a relatively small part of an area which is largely moor and rough grazing. In distant geological time the position was very probably, indeed almost certainly, quite different. Then this whole region was very likely covered in primevel forest and Dartmoor, today renowned more for its bogs, would not have been the only waterlogged waste to have originated through indiscriminate felling of timber. The same was probably true of Cannock Chase and much of the moorland of Scotland. The description on Exmoor as a 'forest' comes in for much the same sort of criticism and for much the same reasons.

In the Midlands the Forest of Arden is sometimes alleged to

have been no more than a 'geogrpahical expression' bearing no relation to the real character of the region it was said to cover. It is more than probable that much of this forest disappeared well before much other Midland woodland, for the neighbouring Worcestershire forests of Horewell and Feckenham seem to have remained long after the bulk of Arden had vanished. However, when compared to Dartmoor and Exmoor, Arden can be said to have existed as a true forest well into historical times. Yet, like the Weald, much of it went as the countryside became increasingly agricultural. Industrial needs probably accounted for some loss of woodland – but the needs of agricultural settlement probably spelt Arden's doom quite early on. However, Warwickshire still remains an extensively wooded area – unlike the moorland 'forests' – especially in the area south of Coventry. If the former forest has gone there is a density of woodland that seems firmly to imply its former existence.

Lying on the Lancashire – Yorkshire border, though in fact most of its area is in the West Riding, the Forest of Bowland is another moorland 'forest' again deriving its name not because of woodland, but because it was a medieval royal chase. Today woodland is sparse in this upland region, though it is to be found in the valley of the River Ribble and in Wharfedale, notably at Oxember Wood some five miles north-west of Settle and at Colt Park. Unlike the moorland forests of Exmoor and Dartmoor it is less likely that the Forest of Bowland was an afforested region even in distant times. Lying so close to the Pennines it would seem to have been moorland since long before the medieval kings began to interest themselves in the pleasures of the chase. Parts of it are now covered by dangerous mosses or bogs and even the kings hunting from nearby Lancaster must have found it hazardous to follow their favourite sport.

Because three of these 'forest' areas, Exmoor, Dartmoor and Bowland contain so many similarities it may be best to consider first the one rogue elephant amongst this collection, the Forest of Arden. Here, as in the case of the others, we are obviously not going to discover forest crafts, forest industry or forest pursuits for the simple reason that there is no longer any forest in which to find them.

Yet the Forest of Arden does survive – not in a growing state it is true, but in the timber-frames of so many buildings in the area. There are to be found splendid half-timbered buildings in almost all the Arden villages and equally in its major towns, Stratford-upon-Avon, Alcester and Bidford-on-Avon. Places such as Shakespeare's birthplace and the half-timbered Garrick Inn in Stratford have been well discussed by a whole army of writers and it is no function of mine to add to vast amount of eulogising that has gone on about the Bard, the Avon and the delights of Stratford.

Like Arden the Forest of Exmoor is rather deficient in trees and has been for many centuries. It has probably been basically moorland since before the coming of the Romans. In the early seventeenth century the forest is described as being without woodland cover, being moorland "time out of mind used for the pasture of great numbers of sheep, cattle and horse beasts". Toward the end of the same century we find that "the Forest or reputed Forest is a very barren place and very full of Boggs". Roads across the moor were almost non-existent and there were few who would venture across it without a guide for fear of being trapped in the bogs. In 1648 someone was foolhardy enough to attempt to cross the moor alone. Later one of his would-be rescuers tells that "he and another were sent into the Forest on the information of two travellers to save a person's life, who was then dying in the Forest; when they reached the dying man, finding him frozen to the ground and past hope of recovery, they left him. He was afterwards buried by the Forester in Withypool churchyard." The office of Forester mentioned in this account does not refer to an official who had anything to do with woodlands but rather to one charged with collecting the royal dues from those pasturing their cattle on the moor. Withypool was the settlement closest to the centre of the moor.

By 1814 there were a grand total of thirty-eight trees in the Forest of Exmoor – and all but one of these grew around Simonsbath farmhouse which stood almost in the middle of the moor. However, Simonsbath House, as it was originally known, had only been built by Janes Boevey in 1654 and the trees there had been planted since the area around had been enclosed to form a small farm. By 1814 this house, once described as "ye Capitall massuadge or dwelling house att Symmonsbath in Exmore Chase", was the local inn. In 1795 it is described as being "licensed and frequented as an Inn" and had been so for the past six years. It was also the home of the deputy foresters who occupied it as tenants. However, it was to remain the centre of local forest administration. The forest however, was not to exist as a crown forest for much longer. In 1819 it was broken up and enclosed, the largest single portion, the King's Inclosure, coming into the ownership of John Knight who had ambitious plans to turn a large area of the moor into profitable farming land. With the purchase of various other areas of Exmoor, John Knight ultimately came to be the owner of some four-fifths of the former Forest of Exmoor.

Knight did not take up permanent residence on the moor until 1827 when he moved into the old house at Simonsbath awaiting completion of a new house in the grounds. His interest in the moorland resulted, around this time, in the creation of some new farmlands and the building of farmhouses. The reclamation activities of Knight and his son Fredric were eventually to result in the creation of sixteen new farms, of roads between Exford and Barnstable and from Simonsbath to Brendon and Challacombe and of the village of Simonsbath itself. Three inns were also built on the fringe of the moorland – the Acland Arms, first licensed in 1825, was long believed to have been a centre of the local smuggling trade. It lay just within the Somerset boundary and thus was beyond the jurisdiction of the local Devon authorities. Moreover, it was a long way from the centres of Somerset administration and it is said that it was for long used as a distributive centre for smuggling goods landed on the coast between Porlock and Coombe Martin. Conveniently positioned at the junction of two old pack-horse roads it would have been well placed for its purpose.

The Knights were to lay out considerable sums on draining, fencing and cultivating part of the moor and their efforts were successful in some areas. However, the centre of the old forest still remains much as it must have appeared a thousand years ago. It was almost not the case, for after John Knight's death, three large mining companies were to begin operations on the moor. These were the Ulverstone Company, the Dowlais Iron Company and the Plymouth Iron Company – the latter with headquarters at Myrthyr Tydfill. However, the initial bores proved insubstantial – though not until after the companies had each spent large sums in exploration and other work. Traces of their work remain today, notably a row of ruined miners' cottages at Cornham Ford and the line of the 'tram road' made to carry the ore to Porlock Weir.

Before leaving Exmoor it is perhaps only right to point out that this vast tract of non-forest moorland was once to have a connection with the woodland forest lands of Dean. This was through James Boevey the original builder of Simonsbath House. Boevey had a sister Joanna who, in 1622, married Abraham Clarke then the owner of Flaxley Abbey, as the remains of the former Cistercian Abbey near Cinderford continued to be called. On the death of Abraham Clarke, in 1683 the Abbey passed to James Boevey's son, William, whose wife Catherine survived him and was the "perverse widow" of Steele's *Sir Roger de Coverley*.

It is also worth mentioning, I think, that James Boevey, for all his Norman-French sounding name – which was pronounced Boovy – was not of ancient aristocratic stock. He was the son of a French Huguenot, Andrew Boeve of Courtai in Flanders who had been brought to England at the age of seven to escape the persecutions of the Duke of Alva in the Low Countries. In 1660 he entered himself at the Inner Temple and his life, in London, was that of a lawyer and merchant – primarily concerned with foreign trade. Pepys seems to make a reference to him in 1688 when he records:

> I met with Sir Richard Browne, and he took me to dinner with him to a new tavern, above Charing Cross, where some clients of his did give him a good dinner, and good company; among others, one Bovy, a solicitor, and lawyer and merchant all together, who hath travelled very much, did talk some things well.

Like the Knights James Boevey also had plans to reclaim much of Exmoor for agriculture. But his efforts were not very successful and he spent much of his time at Simonsbath House writing books on philosophy.

Lancashire had two 'forests' very similar to that of Exmoor, but which were destined to develop in very different ways. The Forest of Bowland was to remain pastoral – as it still is – while the Forest of Rossendale was to become a centre of the textile industry. In the seventeenth century the Rossendale region began to develop as a hand-loom weaving centre – a cottage industry which had spread across the border from the West Riding of Yorkshire. Gradually the scattered settlements of small-holdings began to grow and by the opening of the eighteenth century Rossendale was poised to develop as a new industrial region. Technically it might be correct to treat it here as a 'forest' development. However, such a consideration would lie outside the scope of this book.

The Forest of Bowland was a different matter altogether. If the Forest of Rossendale could, at one time, be said to have been rather remote then Bowland was, by comparison, positively isolated. Bowland was to remain non-industrial and today is largely given over to dairy and sheep farming. Like Exmoor, Bowland has been largely moor since historic times and has probably not born a forest cover since the Bronze Age. The highest ground is peat-covered and is largely uninhabited. Like Rossendale it retains the name 'forest' because it was once used as a medieval hunting chase. In medieval times there was very little settlement in Bowland and the sparseness of such settlement accounts for the fact that there grew up no recognizable market centre for the region. Bowland came to rely for its livelihood on a system of subsistence farming which gradually widened to take in the making of cheese and the selling of cattle to the towns of industrial Lancashire. In the middle years of the nineteenth century life was still following an age-old pattern for there was no road system which had been turn-piked and the population still lived largely on the traditional diet of whey, oatcakes and salted meat. Villages, most often hamlets, did establish themselves in the Bowland region – but they were to be disastrously effected by the rural drift of population to the towns.

Bowland's major agricultural activity was to become the raising of cattle which were largely bought by farmers on the Lancashire Fylde lowlands who, first using them for dairying, later fattened them for slaughter. This did not provide a very remarkable livelihood and, with the attractions of industry near at hand, Bowland's population began to fall as men left for the factories. Even up until the early 1960s the population in this area of Lancashire was still falling at a time when commuter and retired settlers were tending to push up the population figures in many areas of rural England, especially those relatively near to large towns. Today there has been some change in this situation. But Bowland remains dominantly pastoral and sparsely populated. Here and there ruined cottages and smallholdings bear witness to the exodus which marked the century between 1860 and 1960.

The retired in search of the picturesque have been moving into Devon – even onto Dartmoor – for a long time. They, like most visitors, value its untouched landscape and few may know that almost two centuries ago it was being confidently predicted that the 'waste' would soon be under the plough and yielding drops of the finest wheat. In fact, the moor of the Royal Forest of Dartmoor is today very much as it was toward the end of the eighteenth century, indeed it is very much in the state it was more than a thousand years ago.

However, it was once a royal chase and when the area officially ceased to be royal forest in the reign of Henry III, the old appellation remained and has lingered on into our own day.

In those days there certainly was some woodland on the moor – and in this respect it was certainly dissimilar to Exmoor. The most notable remains of what may once have been an original forest cover for at least a part of the moorland are to be found at Wistman's Wood, a little to the west of Postbridge on the Moretonhampstead-Princetown Road. The character of this wood recalls some modern children's fable created by Tolkien or C.S. Lweis. Its gnarled and stunted oaks may be one of the few surviving remnants of an oakwood forest of far more noble character which once spread across Dartmoor before the long-ago days of permanent climatic change. Its centre was burnt out toward the end of the last century following a picnicker's camp-fire – but this central clearing now serves only to further emphasize its eerie atmosphere. It would be a hardy character who would wish to camp overnight in the middle of the wood. Other woodland is to be found in the present-day moor notably Holne Wood, lying not far from Wistman's Wood, and also in the upper valley of the Dart, Black Tor Copse lying a few miles south of Okehampton and Yarner Wood on the fringe of the Bovey Valley.

Elsewhere we are left with what remains of the stones and crosses which once marked the boundary of the official forest. Some Dartmoor crosses also existed as guide-posts, and because these and the boundary markers did not serve a primarily religious function, they were largely to survive the iconoclasms that characterized the Reformation and the Commonwealth.

One of the oldest forest-boundary crosses still surviving is Siward's Cross some two-and-a-half miles south of Princetown. It is sometimes referred to as Nun's Cross. On the eastern face is the inscription "SIWARD". On the western side is the inscription "BOC LOND" and a small cross. This cross is mentioned in the foundation deeds of Buckland Abbey and served the dual purpose of boundary sign and guide-post.

Mention of Buckland Abbey brings us to the place of the medieval Church on Dartmoor. Especially in the southern region of the moor the religious houses were largely responsible for creating the medieval system of trackways, though the ancient track known as Abbot's Way was probably in existence long before the monks came here. In this region of the moor there were four religious houses Buckland, Buckfast, Plympton and Tavistock. Buckland was founded in the late thirteenth century and Buckfast more than two centuries earlier in the time of Cnut. Buckfast is one of those which is now re-occupied – this time by monks of the Benedictine order. Rebuilding work was begun in 1882 and the monastery was consecrated in 1932.

Both Plympton and Tavistock monasteries began life in the tenth century. Tavistock was to become extremely wealthy and contributed greatly to the opening up of the moor for agricultural purposes. The monastery of Plympton once exercised jurisdiction over the land now occupied by nearby Plymouth. All shared in the fate of England's religious houses at the time of the Reformation. Most of the lands of Tavistock passed into the hands of the Russells, later Dukes of Bedford, who did not relinquish their hold on them until shortly before the beginning of the First World War.

Traditionally Dartmoor has been one of England's most isolated areas. To the south-east there is the major city of Exeter and to the south-west the port of Plymouth. The communication between these two has traditionally skirted the southern fringe of the moor. To the north the A30 London-Penzance road, which reaches Exeter via Okehampton and Crediton, provides the boundary for both the north and east, while the road from Plymouth via Tavistock to Okehampton could be said to provide the western boundary. On the fringes of the actual moor there are three major settlements in Bovey Tracey, Moreton Hampstead and Ashburton.

The mysterious, ominous atmosphere has exercised the imagination of many writers and most notably, perhaps, that of Conan Doyle. Here he set *The Hound of the Baskervilles*. However, Dartmoor does throw up legends of its own. There is, for example, that of the Hairy Hand. The genre is not limited to Dartmoor, nor to Devon, though it does not seem to crop up beyond the South-west. In one way or another the Hairy Hand seems to have been making its appearance on the moor for at least the last three hundred years, and probably for much longer. All accounts say that the hand is all that appears and that it is not accompanied by the rest of a human body. From the eighteenth century we have the account of a man who found his horse out of control on the moor when the reins were seized by a phantom hand. It was only with the greatest fortune that he prevented himself from being killed.

A similar story comes from the twenties of our own century when a motorcyclist careered out of control on one of the moor roads. He was not killed, but badly shaken up and later declared that the handle-bars had been wrenched from his grasp by a hand against which he had been powerless to struggle. The hand had turned the bike toward the roadside while he had been travelling at speed and a crash had been inevitable. More recently there is the account of a woman who was spending a night on Dartmoor with her husband in a caravan. In the middle of the night she was awakened by a strange sound and looking up saw that a hand had come into the caravan through the open window above her husband's head. However her waking seems to have disturbed it and it withdrew into the darkness. Waking her husband they both went outside with torches, but could see any sign of anyone. Although this is rather different to the two stories of the hand causing accidents on the highway it would seem to be the same-manifestation.

Even more than Exmoor, Dartmoor was – and occasionally still is – a grim place for the stranger travelling alone. In fact, in the days before modern transport, many people living on the fringes of the moor made quite a respectable living as guides. Nor was the moor really to be opened up by the coming of the railways. Like earlier forms of communication they tended to skirt the moor itself, the main lines west of Exeter running southward to Plymouth and northward via Crediton and Okehampton to Plymouth again. Branch lines were built, but they have all gone and it seems strange to think that, under the aegis of the Great Western Railway, they were all running fitfully at the end of the Second World War. Now, although the railway lines still girdle Dartmoor, the Dart Valley Railway is the only branch line operating in the Dartmoor area – and this only as a summer-months holiday attraction at fares which are generally far too expensive to appeal to the pockets of local folk.

Just as on Exmoor James Boevey and the Knights had entertained ambitious plans for reclamation and development, so their ardour was to be repeated on Dartmoor by Thomas Tyrwhitt. Tyrwhitt was Lord Warden of the Stannaries, private secretary to the Prince of Wales and at one time M.P. for Plymouth. Tyrwhitt's reclamation project began in 1785 and was centred upon the creation of Prince's Town – named out of deference to the Prince of Wales – and the idea of linking this to Plymouth by a horse-hauled railway. There already existed a road nearby running from Tavistock to Moreton Hampstead and Tyrwhitt linked Princetown to this by the construction of a road to Two Bridges.

The town did come into being – or rather the hamlet that was to form the nucleus of the later development – but Tyrwhitt's ambition to grow extensive crops of wheat and to found a linen industry which would use locally grown flax came to nothing. By 1805 Princetown consisted of a few cottages, an inn and a toll-gate which functioned rather as an ornament than as a commercial enterprise. Tyrwhitt, however, did not give up. When the problem of where to put the growing number of French prisoners of war came up he was only too happy to tell the Transport Board – which strangely enough was charged with the responsibility of sick and wounded seamen-prisoners of war – that the Prince of Wales was willing for any part of the moor to be used to build a prison. But Tyrwhitt's concern was with Princetown and this he suggested as a likely location. Thus the prison came to Dartmoor, seeing its first batch of French prisoners in 1809. It was however, far from complete and it was the prisoners themselves who, over the next six years, largely finished off the job. Incidentally, they also built the parish church, working for a rate of 6d per day.

From Thomas Tyrwhitt's point of view, the end of the Napoleonic Wars and the subsequent repatriation of the settlement's prisoners, was untimely. Something had to be found to give his settlement a new lease of life. One suggestion which at first looked quite promising was that the building became the early nineteenth-century equivalent of a modern industrial training centre for the child beggars, thieves and prostitutes who then infested the London streets. But the idea came to nothing. Tyrwhitt now returned to the promotion of Princetown as an agricultural centre with granite quarrying added as a further possibility. It was the latter which saved the day. A horse-hauled railway was completed in 1823. When Thomas Tyrwhitt died in 1833 Princetown was booming as a result of the granite quarrying and he probably believed that his project for establishing a town on the moorland had at last been vindicated.

But the granite boom was short lived. Within a decade the quarries were silent and Princetown was being described as a scene of "utter desolation". In 1846 the buildings were to be taken over by the British Patent Naptha Company which had plans for the production of naphtha from Dartmoor peat. It was only a limited success. The naphtha produced was found to have little commercial value and the company went into liquidation. But Princetown was on the verge of salvation. In

1846 the transportation system was suspended and various efforts were made to provide penal substitutes in the hulks moored off Bermuda and Gibralta. But this was no more than a temporary expedient. England could no longer dump its convicted men on other parts of the world. The government of the day began to look around for any place that could house the criminals it could no longer transport to Botany Bay.

One of the places they chose was Princetown and the future of Thomas Tyrwhitt's town was assured. The first convicts arrived in 1850 and their successors have been arriving ever since. Escapes were fairly frequent in the early days, but the majority were to be beaten by the bad weather and the inhospital moorland terrain. There were successful escapes however, one of the most remarkable being by two twelve-year-olds in the early 1860s. These got away due to the simple fact that the prison had never been designed to hold children and they bade it farewell merely by squeezing through the bars. After this they scaled the boundary wall and clambered down its outside by a rope. They were never heard of again and if they did not in fact succeed in leaving the moor their end must surely have come in the Dartmoor bogs. At all events, their bodies were never found.

In the region of Princetown a considerable area of moorland has long since been converted into agricultural land by the labour of the prisoners and Thomas Tyrwhitt's dream of a reclaimed Dartmoor has at least come to a limited realization. There have been rumours in recent years that the great prison will close. It may yet do so. But if it ever does then Princetown is likely to close with it.

Princetown, of course, is not the only settlement on the moor, though it is its largest one. Dartmoor still has its hill-farmers, living in inevitably isolated farmhouses which during winter are often cut off from the outside world by the snows which blanket the moor. In earlier days preparations were made for these winters by an annual stocking up of food and fuel. Nonetheless, it was a rare Dartmoor winter which did not claim its dead. Nowadays relief has often been brought by helicopter. However, Dartmoor winters have not deterred the retired from flocking into moorland cottages – though it has to be admitted that most prefer something in or near one of the fringing villages or towns. Dartmoor winters probably help to ensure that their stay is rarely a long one.

Dartmoor is today a tourist centre comparable in popularity with the Peak District, the Lakes and the Cotswolds. If tourist Dartmoor has a centre then this must be Widecombe. Its church, with a tower more than a hundred feet high, is dedicated to St Pancras. The fair is still held annually in September though it must be much changed since Tom Cobley's day.

The moor, however, is perhaps not quite the isolated mass it once was. Cars spin along its roads and the mast of BBC television extends a thin finger upward from North Hessary Tor bringing the outside world to even the most isolated of snowbound winter cottages. In many cases children no longer attend the small village schools but leave in the mornings via school-bus for the larger schools of the border towns. But, though occasionally flirting with the present, in the mists of darkness and the white shroud of winter, Dartmoor still seems to belong to a primeval past.

9

The Surviving Evidence

As has been said earlier, since at least the middle of the seventeenth century, England has had the peculiar distinction of being Europe's least afforested country. Yet its remaining forest areas tend to be relatively well-defined, especially those now forming part of the woodlands under the management of the Forestry Commission.

England's two largest forest areas are now – and have been for the past three centuries – the New Forest and the Forest of Dean. The New Forest is just over 67,000 acres in extent – although not all this is under timber. In the Forest of Dean itself woodland accounts for some 21,000 acres, though other nearby woodland and a certain amount of rough grazing land, lying outside the actual boundary of the forest, considerably increases the area of what could be called tourist Dean.

Both Dean and the New Forest are important parts of the English timber industry. But here we shall be considering them and the other major areas of English forest largely from the point of view of the visitor. The New Forest lying near to London and the Home Counties attracts the largest number of visitors to any forest area, while those who visit Dean seem to be roughly equally divided between those from London and the Midlands. Many of the smaller forest regions would seem to exercise a markedly local appeal from the point of view of their visiting population. It is very much Londoners who visit Epping and its associated forest of Hainault while Midlanders form the bulk of visitors to forests such as Charnwood, Wyre, Sherwood and Cannock Chase. Northerners largely visit Delamere and the Fountains Abbey Woods – the remnant of the Forest of Knaresborough – but then they have the dales and fells as well as the extensive Forestry Commission plantations that form the East Yorkshire Forest and the Border Forest Park.

In fact it would appear that it is the smaller Midland forests which are under greatest pressure. Here there are few other 'outdoor playgrounds'. The region is, for most, too far from the sea for the casual day-outing and it does not have the downland of the South-east nor the moorlands of the North and West. There does exist the open land of the Long Mynd and the Clee Hills, but most such areas are smaller including, for example, the Clent and Lickey Hills. With these exceptions the weekending Midlander tends to seek his leisure at the canal or riverside or, increasingly, to make for nearby woodland. Higher petrol costs can only intensify this trend to take one's recreation as near to hand as possible.

Of the Midland forests it is Cannock which has proved most popular, followed by the smaller forest of Wyre. Both draw their visitors largely from the industrial Black Country of South Staffordshire and Northern Worcestershire, a visiting tide which especially at summer weekends and Bank Holidays also spills out to leave its marks on the forests of Rock and Kinver.

The popularity of Cannock Chase has created some severe conservation problems for some parts of it have become so frequented during the summer months that problems of soil erosion have arisen – in a different sphere the same problem affects some parts of our fore-shore where erosion has been caused by the continual trampling of sand dunes which has allowed the sand to be blown further inshore. Parts of the chase have become so popular that, in what are now normal conditions, there is no hope of vegetation growing to provide the soil with its necessary protective and adhesive cover. In places this has led to deep channels developing on slopes in the aftermath of heavy rainfall and, at one time, parts of the chase were in danger of becoming a land-use nightmare. The problem has been partly solved by temporarily fencing off certain areas and limiting access to others on a rotation basis. By this process the affected parts of the chase may be restored to normal growth within a few years.

The motor-car can also pose a problem. In certain areas, notably those under the control of the National Parks, attempts are being made to ease the impact of the car by closing certain roads to traffic during the summer months. This follows the successful closure of the Peak District's Goyt Valley road in 1969 which was a pilot experiment in this form of traffic control. In areas under the management of the Forestry Commission a solution is being sought in the creation of more carparks. Ideally, as in the Forest of Wyre, these are small parks at various points rather than large parking areas at one or two main sites. There is obviously a limit, however, to the amount of parking that can be assimilated into the forest areas, especially the smaller woodlands. The time cannot be far away when a halt has to be called to the provision of more car-parking space.

In most of the forests the danger of fire is an increasing hazard. Various preventive measures are taken including the use of Japanese larch as a fire-screen – this being both a difficult wood to burn and one which permits the minimal growth of ground vegetation – the erection of watch-towers, the creation of fire-belts – often with the aid of chemicals which either destroy or limit vegetation – and by the introduction of increasingly sophisticated fire-fighting machinery. It is the hazard of fire as much as the need to remove felled trees, that has resulted in the creation of the majority of forest roads. One major cause of past forest fires has been removed in recent years as diesel and electric locomotives have replaced coal-fired ones. But road-side hazards, from such things as picnic primus-stoves, have increased and with the general opening up of woodland to the public, there has been an all-round increase in risk. A few fires are begun maliciously, but most are caused by accident, not so much by the carelessly dropped cigarette but rather from the smashed bottle whose pieces can intensify sunlight and cause conflagrations in the under-growth months after they have been dropped. Unless such fires can be got to quickly an immense amount of destruction can be caused. In such areas as Cannock Chase fires can burn for days, even if confined to a relatively small area, for they are not so much surface as underground fires burning away at the peat-like earth that makes up many forest floors.

But, leaving aside the threats which imperil our remaining

woodland, let us consider what we will be getting for our day, weekend or fortnight in the woods. The day-tripper remains the basic visitor to all our woodlands. As would be expected he and his family are the bulk of overnight guests at most woodland hotels and guest houses. But the forests also attract the coach-tour operators, these mostly patronizing the New Forest and the Forest of Dean, in the case of the latter usually bracketing it with the Wye Valley and Symonds Yat. Coaches also ply to Sherwood, throwing in the Dukeries and to Cranbourne Chase as part of 'Hardy's Wessex'. Long-stay visitors tend to be largely of the caravaning fraternity and the Caravan Club has a number of sites in most forest areas. There are also the youth hostels for more adventurous souls and canvas, camp-fires, cocoa and sleeping-bags for the members of the Boys' Brigade, Scouts and similar school-holiday organizations. This is not to say that sophistication is entirely absent from the greenwood – the Forest of Dean's Speech House is as good a hotel as could be found anywhere as are a number of those in and around the New Forest. Nonetheless *à la carte* meals, expensive wines and room service do, at first sight, seem a little at variance with nature trails, wild ponies and children who think it is a good idea to paddle in small streams with their shoes on.

Nowadays the average visitor to the major forest areas would seem to want a fair measure of history mixed in with his pilgrimage to the trees. But the diet which was once meted out to his Victorian predecessors has been found wanting in this more democratic age. Tales of William Rufus, and Robin Hood together with locally set novels, copiously researched guidebooks and long, leisurely walks through secluded glades have given way to a growing interest in how ordinary men and women gained their livelihood in the forest. In other parts of the country this new interest has been partly catered for by the growth of industrial museums and the Forest of Dean – as one of the oldest industrial centres in England – now boasts its own industrial museum at Park End.

At Park End some of the museum's exhibits are in working order and there are plans to restore some of the old railway track and to create a complete steam and industrial museum. As far as possible this will demonstrate most of the working processes of the former major industries of the Dean area.

Away from the industrial relics of Park End there survives historical evidence of a more 'romantic' variety. The seventeenth-century Speech House still annually preserves the fiction of being the ancient Verderers' Court when the dining room is ceremoniously opened and closed for legal business. The ceremony takes no more than five minutes and the public is not admitted. Away from the present forest area proper St Briavel's castle is also not open to the public. The castle, which was once the headquarters of the Constable and into whose dismal dungeons offenders against the Forest Laws were once cast, now functions as a youth hostel. It can, of course, still be looked at, but as St Briavel's – though once the centre of the Hundred of St Briavel's and therefore of the forest – now lies someway beyond the official boundary of the forest it tends to be bypassed by many visitors.

But if the casual visitor is unable to get into the Norman castle at St Braivel's there is nothing to prevent him walking along the stretch of Roman road which survives near Blackpool Bridge. This piece of road was once part of a longer link that ran from Lydney to Micheldean providing the iron of Dean with its route to the sea even in those far off times. Not all that long ago some of this ancient road was mistakenly tarred and resurfaced by the local council. It has since been fully restored.

If one is on the look-out for industrial history – other than that being reassembled at Park End – it is quite literally to be found all over the Forest. Though it would be advisable to tread carefully to avoid slipping into some of it. Abandoned collieries and mine-workings abound – though it has to be admitted that it would take a committed romantic to conjur beauty out of some of the scenes.

This may be the place to point out that the Forest of Dean contributed a man of genius to England's industrial past. The man was Sir John Wyntour, who has already been met devastating Dean's seventeenth-century timber supply. It was this same Sir John who is said to have invented a process for "charring sea-coal to burn out the sulphur and render it sweet". This was none other than the production of coked coal. Wyntour is said to have been working on the process while imprisoned in the Tower of London under the Commonwealth. When he returned to Dean it would seem unlikely that he did not put his discovery to use. However, it would not seem to have survived the general closure of the Dean iron industry during the latter years of the reign of Charles II.

But the sights of Dean are not limited to remnants of its industrial past – it has a considerable industrial present, though trading estates are usually the sort of things most visitors are racing away from. But there is also history from an age we can happily imagine as golden and which, to our imaginations at least, can certainly seem more substantial than that of steam. Not only does Dean have a Roman road – as well as Roman iron-workings near Scowles and others now virtually unidentifiable because they have been persistently raked over in later times – but near Lydney, it also has the ruins of a Roman temple. Strictly speaking this is a Romano-British temple for it was dedicated to the river-god of the Silures, Noddens.

Not far away, within sight of the new Severn Bridge, one traditional occupation survives. Lave-fishing may have an ancestry reaching back to Celtic, pre-roman times. The lave-fishermen are salmon fishers in a commercial way, doing most of their work at night in and on the banks of the Severn estuary. Their large nets are in the form of scoops carried at the end of long poles. Spotting the tell-tale sign of rippled water made by the salmon the lave-fishermen dash into the water and, when near enough, thrust their nets into the water and rapidly following the movements of the fish scoop it into the net. The salmon moves faster than the fisherman – but experience makes up the deficiency. However, were it not for the scarcity of salmon and the high prices they nowadays command as a luxury dish lave-fishing would most surely have gone the way of most ancient occupations.

There still survive a few Dean free-miners who, irrespective of the size of their pits, hack a precarious living underground. Their pits are the only ones in England to have escaped nationalization – although they are now limited in number. Charcoal burners of the traditional brand – the original colliers – do not survive. In their place is a charcoal-making factory which, amongst other things, supplies the art world with its broad black lines. Of iron-workers there are none – strange when it is discovered that there were sixty-two itinerant forges in the forest as long ago as 1282. It was iron, of course, which founded the industrial prosperity of Dean. There is still iron to be found for the deposits were never worked out – though it would now seem to be uneconomic to contemplate reviving the local industry.

However, there are still ship-badgers. This is the name given to the part-time shepherds who superintend the forest sheep – 'Ship' because this is the forest pronounciation of sheep, 'badgers' because one of their tasks, with the aid of their collie, is to badger sheep from other flocks from mingling with their own. Most ship-badgers are not shepherds in the strict sense of the word for they own their own flocks which generally number between two and four hundred sheep. Very often the ship-badger is also a free-miner – and where he is not he is usually the descendant of one – and in times past the flock provided the only means of supplementing his meagre income from the mine. The sheep do not graze in Dean by right but, it would seem, by privelege from the Crown as owner of the forest. Nor do sheep graze all over Dean – though it would seem that they graze, or rather forage, all over Cinderford. Certain areas of the forest where there is new growth are enclosed against the sheep – in the time of Charles II this was done by erecting walls which can still be found in some areas. At any one time sheep can graze roughly half the area of the actual woodland.

Mention of boundary walls brings us to the greatest of all English border defences, Offa's Dyke (Hadrian's Wall was built before there were any Englishmen in existence). The dyke, which ran almost the whole length of the Welsh Border, began at Tiddenham which then formed the southern extremity of the forest. Within the bounds of the old forest the great earthwork can still be traced on the left bank of the Wye – though it has to be admitted that the Dyke does not survive at its best here.

It was the dyke which really cut off the forest's Celtic population from those to the west and which, in time, produced the individually regional phenomena of 'the forester'. Confined within this woodland bowl of iron and oak there was little communication with the outside world for most forest folk – but what there was came to be eastward toward Gloucester and England rather than toward Wales. It cannot be claimed that the foresters became Anglicized, but the English from east of severn were to mingle with the forest folk to produce a hybrid population that was almost a race in itself. Some writers have claimed that the native population has remained almost exclusively Celtic. Temperamentally this may be true, for the forester is as musical as the Welshman and has a natural appreciation of poetry that is, at least, un-English. But racially this contention would be far more difficult to uphold. Cymric features may be common but, especially in the north of the forest around Micheldean and Ruadean the traditional blonde and blue eyed descendant of the Saxon is relatively numerous. In the matter of ethnic origins, especially in England, it is dangerous even to generalize. Yet the average native of Dean does appear to share with many of the Cymru a smallness of stature irrespective of other physical details. I was once told that this was the product of a peculiarly local evolution, as no one of more than average size could have been expected to work the warrens that comprised the Dean free-mines. That explanation, however I think needs to be taken with a rather large pinch of salt.

The 'forester' also acquired a reputation for other peculiarities. But much of this was certainly fable born in the minds of outsiders who almost invariably conjured up tales about communities which were so seemingly insular and exclusive as those of Dean. In some cases the myths were based in fact – but they owed an equal inspiration to the fear and envy of the foresters' neighbours. The foresters certainly enjoyed a reputation as fighting men which, in many ways, still survives. Undoubtedly this went back to the distant days when the miners fought in the service of England's medieval kings but, in later times, it would have been reinforced by such events as the Bread Riots and the enclosure riots of the late eighteenth and early nineteenth centuries. Again, despite its woodland, Dean was an industrial region and, economically at least, the rural worker has generally been intimidated by his industrial counterpart.

This reputation for lawlessness was reinforced, until the mid-eighteenth century, by Dean remaining a 'godless' region, largely without the edifices of church or chapel and the Anglican Church did not begin to make its presence felt in the forest until the third decade of the nineteenth century. Dean's repute as a nest of fighting-cocks led to the birth of some strange tales concerning the foresters in neighbouring localities. The virility of the foresters was said to be far greater than that of normal men and, in southern Herefordshire at least, the phrase 'lock up your daughters' seems to have had a special relevance whenever the foresters were about. The foresters were said to be extremely boastful of their sexual prowess, and it was alleged that a forester was capable of fathering a child before he was in his teens. One explanation of this was given in the belief that the foresters, in their medieval fastness, continued in debased form, a version of ancient fertility rites which included wise men, aphrodisiacal concoctions of animal fats, and nights of ritual amongst the young apprentices in their underground caverns. However, it would be difficult to see how any of this could take place in the narrow levels of the actual free mines. Such tales may have had a flimsy basis in fact which, perhaps gave fuel to the ire of a particularly disgruntled and cockolded agricultural worker determined to ensure that he would besmirch the reputation of all foresters because of one's success with his own neglected wife. I must also say that both these tales come from Ross-on-Wye whose older inhabitants to this day, have somewhat ambivalent feelings about the Dean foresters. They are rather similar to the 'poor white' tales of negroes in the Southern States of America – and were, like them, probably born of fear and antagonism. If the foresters ever heard them they probably nodded gravely, said little and later laughed all the way home to Cinderford or Micheldean.

But, if anything remotely resembling this sort of thing ever did take place it was certainly not destined to outlive Dean's occupation by the nineteenth-century church militant. By the early nineteenth century the Church had begun to colonize the forest – up till then the 'forest' churches being limited to those areas which were now beyond the actual woodland, such as St Briavel's and Newland. The perpendicular Newland church is, however, still referred to as 'the cathedral of the Forest' and within is to be found a small, fifteenth-century brass depicting a free-miner with tools and clothing which were hardly to change until the close of the last century. The Newland Oak has reputedly stood for more than six centuries though, in its deformity, it has now reached a most unpleasantly advanced stage of senility. Girded, cossetted and protected the Oak stands in decrepit isolation in the middle of a field. It has of recent years, begun to renew itself, pheonix-like some time after it was almost completely destroyed by lightening. The life of its new sapling will be unavoidably rooted in the traditional associations of the older tree.

Newland has livelier timber associations with the forest for the village is still plentifully surrounded by trees. There are also a number of fine houses and a row of early seventeenth-century almshouses which still serve their original function of providing for the needs of some of the region's older folk. Like St Briavel's and other villages that were once surrounded by forest but which now stand some miles beyond its fringe, Newland offers a sharp contrast with most of the village settlements that grew up later in the woodland areas. The fringe villages are all of some antiquity, whilst the villages of the forest heartland are mostly creations of the late eighteenth and nineteenth centuries with a tendency to straggle – their haphazard, vaguely industrial meanness relying for its redemption upon their sylvan environs. However, they are not entirely without charm, especially in these days of characterless, geometric towns and suburbs. But only at the risk of the withdrawal of one's poetic license could they be labelled picturesque.

Another of Dean's fringe settlements Lydney was, of course, home to Sir John Wyntour. Besides his felling and smelting activities in the forest Sir John was to bring Lydney to prominence as a Royalist stronghold during the Civil War. This was especially so after Bristol had fallen to the Parliamentary forces. Then the Forest of Dean became a Royalist fortress garrisoned by troops under the command of Sir John and Prince Rupert. A little earlier Sir John had fortified his Lydney home, White Cross House, against the forces of Colonel Massey, the Parliament's Governor of Bristol. The house had been built by Sir John's father, Sir

William Wyntour who had been Admiral of the White in the victory over the Spanish Armada off Gravelines. During Sir John's absence it was to be surrounded by Massey's troops and was called upon to surrender. But when Massey discovered that it was being defended only by Sir John's wife and a small force of family servants he courteously withdrew – promising that he would return to engage Sir John when their forces would be more equal.

Sir John had already been victorious in a number of skirmishes against Massey's troops. But these, which included minor 'battles' at Newnham and Westbury, had been small-scale affairs and Sir John sensibly doubted if he could hope to win the field against a full detachment of troops from Gloucester. Accordingly he decided to burn out White Cross House to prevent it falling into the hands of his enemies – an example of self-sacrifice and disregard for financial advantage that was at complete variance with all his former activities in Dean.

In course of time Lydney did indeed fall to Massey and, retreating from the town, Wyntour and Prince Rupert were to find themselves hemmed in by their enemies on the Beachley peninsula. It is here, where the Wye enters the Severn Estuary just beyond Chepstow, that the Severn Bridge now soars above the waters to link South Wales to the West. Wyntour decided to reconnoitre the investing lines and succeeded in slipping past them. He was, however, spotted by a troop of Ironsides who gave chase to the lone horseman. Inexplicably it must have seemed, Wyntour now galloped full tilt in the direction of Lancaut, a hilltop almost encircled by a loop of the Wye. The two-hundred foot drop above the river is still known as Wyntour's Leap and was certainly enough to bring his pursuers to a halt. But Sir John had not leapt the Wye. A few yards from the cliff-top a well-screened path led down through trees to the water's edge. It was this path which Sir John now took. Riding along the riverbank, under cover from the trees, he eventually hailed a small boat. Within sight of his pursuers on the cliff-top he now embarked and was to return to the safety of Beachley.

Some time later Sir John again extricated himself from the Beachley peninsula to become the Royalist governor of

Chepstow castle. But the Royalist cause was now in tatters. Eventually Sir John was to make his way to the Royalist 'capital' of Oxford and was finally to be captured and imprisoned in the Tower. For the last two years of the war he had been the Royalist's greatest champion in the West. It was his tenacity in the Royalist cause and his undoubted self-sacrifice in its defence that did so much to redeem Sir John's reputation in the minds of the foresters – even after the Restoration when he again took up his commercial warfare with the woodlands.

Lydney has been the forest port since Roman times – and maybe even earlier. It catered very largely for the iron and coal trades, for timber felled in the forest for shipbuilding was floated down smaller rivers into the Severn and so to Bristol, foreshadowing the logging techniques that later came to be used in the great North American timber-lands. Both Drake and Raleigh are said to have stayed in the town whilst visiting the forest in connection with the affairs of the navy. In the nineteenth century, Lydney was to be connected to the forest heartland forst by horse-hauled tramways and later by railways. Set partly upon a hillside it is now a rather congested small town lying athwart the main A48 coast road into South Wales. It has a fine church and a number of well proportioned houses of local stone. Its existence as a port is minimal and the nearby Aust-Beachley ferry has ceased to operate since the opening of the Severn roadbridge.

Further along the A48, in the direction of Gloucester, is Blakeney whose chief glory is its orchards of pear trees which almost unite it to the forest lying behind them. A few miles further on is the long street of Newnham which, at its northern end, turns to run alongside the wide, salt-flats of the Severn estuary which, notwithstanding the haze of industry, docks and buildings on the further shore, can be an idyllic sight at the height of summer. In winter however, it can offer the most penetrating of Arctic blasts. The lave-fishermen of the Severn are no doubt duly grateful that their trade is seasonally confined to the months of late Spring and early Summer.

Turning Westward toward the forest from Newnham Littledean is the first village to be reached – though this again also now lies outside the confines of the forest proper. The village was once one of the main centres of forest administration and surviving from this time is the former forest gaol, now put to other uses. In fact, the high walls of the gaol dominate the village and the only prisoner ever known to escape from here was soon recaptured in a nearby outbuilding being rather hampered in further progress by a broken leg. Other survivals include the remains of a monastic grange once in the possession of the monks of Flaxley Abbey. The Abbey was founded in 1140 and grew prosperous as a result of the thirteenth-century iron boom, the monks engaging in the smelting of the iron themselves. Within Flaxley's unpretentious Church is a memorial tablet to Mrs Catherine Boevey, whom Richard Steele was to portray as the widow so assiduously courted by his famous literary creation Sir Roger de Coverley.

Micheldean was once the 'great dean' – the largest town in the forest. Nowadays however, it acts more as a gateway into the forest lands that lie beyond it. Around it however, there are large plum orchards and nearby Blaisdon has given its name to one particular variety, the Blaisdon red. I once knew the foreman of a large horticultural estate whose major ambition in life was to create a new variety of plum. But all his efforts were to no avail. He finally became so embittered by his fruitless task that the nation has cause to be grateful that he did not, in his later years, produce the sourest plum imaginable. The tower of Micheldean church is topped by the most slender of spires rising to what is almost a needle-point and upon which revolves what must be the most wary of vulnerable weathercocks.

At Ruardean the church tower is also topped by a slender spire. Although Ruardean still exists as a mining town it seems somewhat apart from Dean – even more apart than the other forest boundary villages that lie near it. It looks out toward the pastures and woodlands of neighbouring Herefordshire and, in some indefinite way, seems to link itself to the northern landscape.

Nearby is Lydbrook, lying within the bounds of the forest proper with its Church of the Holy Jesus dating from 1851. Shortly after its construction it was described as having been built in, the ultimate of ecclesiastical contradictions, 'the

Geometrical style of Decorated architecture'. Unfortunately for modern Englishmen geometric in architectural terms has come to mean sometning infinitely more severe than will be found at Lydbrook church. On a nearby hillside is an architectural refugee from Hereforeshire, a house of half-timber and red-brick standing upon a substantial stone base. This was once home to the youthful Sarah Siddons whose acting career spanned the forty-five years from 1767 to 1812 when she made her last appearance at Covent Garden. She did not, in fact, die until 1851, after spending a retirement of thirty-nine years and dying at the age of ninety-six.

Sarah lived at Lydbrook with her father and brothers, the famous acting Kembles. Her father, Roger, was originally the head of a group of strolling players mainly composed of members of his own family. One brother, Stephen, was so enormous that it was said he was the only actor in England capable of playing Falstaff without padding. Another brother, Charles, was to leave the profession in favour of the desk-job of Licensor of Plays while the third brother, John, was destined to partner Sarah in her later days of success first at Drury Lane and later at Covent Garden.

Born in Brecon in 1795 Sarah made her first stage appearance at the age of twelve in Harvard's *Charles the First*. Later the family moved from Brecon to Hay-on-Wye and from there came to the house at Lydbrook. It goes without saying that the beauty of a girl destined to dominate the London stage can hardly have left the foresters of Lydbrook unmoved. Nor perhaps, would the preoccupation of her family with the world of words have seemed so unusual for the forester has a ready appreciation of language and has that Celtic mastery of description which can elevate simile and metaphor into a minor art form. Perhaps the young Sarah was not yet so self-assured that she did not blush to hear her beauty compared more than favourably with that of some of the more permanent beauties of the forest. Her stay at Lydbrook however, was to last no longer than a few blossoming summers. Later the family left for Cheltenham and it was from here that she first sprang to national fame opening at Drury Lane in 1775 at Portia in *The Merchant of Venice*. Her first appearance was not a success and it was seven years before she again appeared on the London stage. This time she took the capital by storm and for the next thirty years was to be the undoubted Queen of the English stage.

The church at Drybook was the first to be built within the present-day area of the forest and even now, is often referred to as 'the forest church'. A number of other churches were also built within the forest in the early years of the nineteenth century, including St Paul's, Park End, which was erected in 1822 and St John's, Cinderford, erected in 1844. It should not be thought however, that organized religion was entirely absent from the forest before the arrival of the established Church. Their earlier absence had in many ways assured that the area became a bastion of Non-conformity, one more facet that linked it with the industrial life of other mining areas such as Yorkshire, South Wales and Cornwall. The Non-conformists, as did the later Anglicans, also busied themselves in the provision of education for children and adults alike and this activity assured the social division between the foresters and their often illiterate agricultural neighbours.

South from Drybrook lies one of the modern capitals of the forest – Cinderford, vying with Coleford to be regarded as the Forest's most important local centre. It is quite literally founded on a bed of cinders, charcoal cinders from the time of the Romans and later, and more recently, clinkers from the smelters of the sixteenth and seventeenth centuries which can still be found in the bed of the local stream. The original town grew up mainly as a result of the clearing of the large number of forest squatters, the last dating from the riots of 1831. However, although it had its origins as a squatters' town there is little that is piecemeal about it for, perched upon its hillside, it had compactness imposed upon it. The hillside town has a very un-English feel about it, though if an English comparison is called for then it must be that it is rather like a cross between Devon's Clovelly and Shropshire's Ironbridge though, like all the newer forest towns, it defies the category of the picturesque.

Cinderford's real beauty is not apparent until the hours of evening darkness. The hillside town stretches for roughly two miles in an interlacing series of terraces and small-streets. But at evening these are scarcely visible and are replaced by the grotto effect of street lights and glowing windows. No flat, urban townscape could ever radiate such a feeling of cloistered warmth and home amongst the hills. Perhaps it is a feeling that would not be felt by all that many Englishmen – but the sight must often have induced the isolated depression of *hiraeth* (the nearest English translation for which is homesickness) felt by many an exile from the glow-worm hillsides of South Wales.

The town has another aspect that increases its Welsh affinities. In common with so many of the valley towns it is the uncomplaining home of animals. Not only do sheep enjoy the freedom of Cinderford, but horses as well – though efforts are made to limit the extent of their perambulations. This right of 'pasture' exists because the streets of the town were once part of the forest. But if they stray beyond the limit of former forest land they can be impounded and their owners fined.

A village which shares with Cinderford the distinction of a hillside position is nearby Soudley which lies in the same valley of the river Bideford. In the last century Soudley was an iron-working centre. But its furnaces have long been silent, disused and crumbling, and now the village scatters its way along the valley to form one of the most attractive settlements in the forest. This same quality is absent from Yorkley – whose name is said to derive indirectly from one of the forest walks, York Walk. It is a workaday village, largely originating in the last century and taking, even today, a perverse delight in its apparent isolation. Park End, too, is unremarkable. Yet, it has the remains of its former industrialism, not only in its works but in its workers' cottages. As a settlement its history spans little more than a century. Yet, in the present fashionable interest in the products and symbols of our vanished industrial revolution, it is making a bid for an informed popularity. Doubtless the curiosity of strangers is something its former workers would have at once both marvelled at and resented.

Both Bream and Clearwell are old mining villages, though Clearwell has claims to the larger reputation for it was the site of the Old Sling Mine. Tales are told of the enormous depth of the workings of this mine and the hill of Clearwell Meend, which overlooks the village, must be virtually hollow due to the extent of these workings. The village possesses a wayside cross which at least testifies that it has an ancestory going back into the later centuries of the Middle Ages. Coleford, too, has a past reaching back to medieval times. But, with the boom in coal working and in iron-manufacture in the nineteenth century, it sprouted a ring of suburbs, including Mile End and Coalway that were no less drab and utilitarian than the mining villages. The town treasures the antiquity of its ruined chapel-of-ease, the tower of which still survives, and is at pains to point out that its name derives not from the activities of nineteenth-century miners, but from those of the now-vanished charcoal burners, the original wood-colliers.

A few other settlements lie on the fringes of the forest, such as English Bicknor with another steepled church and the town is worth a visit if only for its air of forgotten, musted charm. There is also Symonds Yat perched above the Wye, which is really a tourist encampment to which the eyes of the traveller have to be averted if he is to enjoy the view of this river gateway. The area could be infinitely expanded by throwing in such places as Chepstow with its mighty fortress or Ross-on-Wye with its spired church finger-pointing skyward above the river and tales of the philanthropic 'Man of Ross'. It would be just as irrelevant to include Winchester in a perambulation of the New Forest.

And so we move to the southern shore. Like the Forest of Dean – which also marches with the Highmeadow Woods, the Forest of Dymock and the Forest of Tintern – the New Forest is also neighboured by other areas of woodland, notably the Forest of Bearse. These, however, we shall leave aside for the moment, while considering the actual attractions of the New Forest itself. It is the largest area of woodland in England and, unlike so many of the others, has not generated for itself more than the faintest trace of an industrial history.

Unlike Dean – whose former administrative centre of St Brivel's now lies beyond the fringe of the present forest – the New Forest has kept its ancient capital, Lyndhurst, at its centre. The most striking building in Lyndhurst is its church, consecrated in 1863, a building in bright red brick further enlivened by the use of yellow. It is a somewhat horrific example of the confidence of the mid-nineteenth century established Church. It is, however, redeemed by an interior which includes stained glasswork by Burne-Jones, Dante Gabriel Rossetti, Ford Maddox Brown and William Morris – a veritable clutch of Pre-Raphelites who presumably, at this point, lived in brotherly harmony. However, the church will probably not detain the visitor, unless there happens to be bad weather. Of greater longevity is the Verderers' Hall which dates from the fourteenth century – though there have been a large number of alterations to its original fabric.

Within the Hall will be found the 'Rufus Stirrup' through which dogs had to pass if they were to avoid being lawed in accordance with the medieval forest laws. Its connection with William Rufus is obscure and very probably completely unfounded. In fact, even the dogs that did not manage to get through the stirrup were not often subject to the cruel practice of lawing. Medieval monarchs, as we keep discovering, were rarely financially secure and preferred to use the stirrup as a taxation instrument. Dogs which did not manage to get through the stirrup were rarely lawed if their owners could afford to pay the 1/- fine.

Adjoining the Verderders' Hall – which is no longer a court of justice – is the King's House, dating largely from its last rebuilding in 1634. This was the equivalent of Dean's St Brival's castle – the seat of local royal administration. In Doomsday Book Lyndhurst is referred to as Linhest – and it has been said that the name derives from the Anglo-Saxon for lime wood. It is only fair to add that some authorities have claimed this cannot be correct on the ground that the lime was not introduced into England until after the Anglo-Saxon period. The lime is, of course, the linden tree.

Having begun in what is almost the central area of the forest it will be wise to stay at the centre and work outward. Not far from Lyndhurst lies Malwood Castle. This is no medieval ruin of fallen ramparts, merely a rising knoll bearing witness to the far-off presence here of a Celtic camp. It is not the only such camp that lies in the northern area of the forest and nearer to the sea on the desolate Plain of Ocknell – which is still marked by the effects of wartime occupation – is Lucas Castle, another hill marking the site of a pre-Roman camp.

Slightly to the north of Lyndhurst is Minstead, a village

which until the 1920s was said to have remained the least altered of all the New Forest villages. It still boasts picturesque thatched cottages and carefully tended flower gardens that are most people's fantasy of bucolic English. Yet even Minstead could not expect to enjoy its once unenvied isolation for ever and the village has been invaded by newer dwellings. Like all the churches of the New Forest – with the exception of that at Beaulieu – that at Minstead stands upon a hill. It dates, in part, from the thirteenth century.

It is in this central area that the visitor is most likely to encounter the shy fallow deer. Indeed, because of its comparative solitude, even in these days of more than a quarter of a million visitors a year, this is the part of the forest where its wildlife traditionally seeks refuge. Up until the early 1900s herons used to nest at Vinney Ridge – but the heronry has long been deserted.

With the exception of Emery Down, which is a residential suburb of Lyndhurst, the second largest settlement in the central forest is Brockenhurst. If Lyndhurst's place-name origins has something to do with linden trees then it may be less than fanciful to suppose that that of Brockenhurst had something to do with badgers. There was a church at 'Broceste' at the time of Doomsday, but the present building dates from the twelfth century, with thirteenth and fourteenth-century additions. The village stands close to the venerable oaklands of Queen's Bower. Brockenhurst was quite small until just after the middle of the last century when the opening of the railway station made it into one of the earliest of the New Forest's commuter villages.

Commuter growth reached the scattered village of Burley somewhat later – largely in the 1920s before anyone had thought of such things as Town and Country Planning Acts, let alone conservation areas. Burley Beacon is reputed to have been the scene of fifteenth-century dragon-slaying. According to "a document of Berkeley Castle, of a date earlier than 1618",

> Sir Moris Barkley the sonne of Sir John Barkley, of Beverston, beinge a man of greater strength and courage, in his tyme there was bred in Hampshire neere Bisterne a devouring Dragon, who

doing much mischief upon men and cattel and could not be destroyed but spoiled many in attempting it, making his den neere unto a Beacon. This Sir Moris Barkley armed himself and encountered with it and at length overcam and killed it but died himself soon after".

There was in fact a Sir Maurice Berkeley who died in 1460 – though perhaps more possibly after a battle with a dragon of the female domestic variety. However, this Sir Maurice was lord of the Manor of Minstead and Brook and there was a Green Dragon Inn here and another at Bisterne. It may be as well to point out that there are a lot of adders in the area of Burley, particularly around Berry Beeches which crown the ridge leading on to Backley Plain.

From Brockenhurst it is easy to reach the villages that line the seaward limit of the New Forest – Beaulieu, Buckler's Hard, Lymington and, on the forest fringe, Milford-on-Sea. The New Forest does, of course, spill over toward Fawley and Southampton Water – though the area east of the Beaulieu River has little of interest compared with that to the west. In fact, as far as possible, the Forestry Commission is at present making every effort to block out the panoramic view of Fawley where they loom a little over-large on the forest vista. To the west is the land of the holly-tree which yields an annual harvest beginning toward the end of November and providing, for countless Londoners and others, the traditional red-berried greenery that decorates the Christmastide home. Some of the land is inclined to be boggy – and, as the bogs can be quite deep, it is best to keep clear of them.

The gem of the forest seaboard is undoubtedly Beaulieu. The abbey was founded by King John in 1205 – who founded rather a lot of religious houses for someone who has since come to enjoy such an evil reputation – and was to be dissolved in 1538 when most of it was pulled down. It was to become the property of the Montague family, who are still in residence and its grounds now contain the National Motor Museum and a collection of amusements, cafeteria and so forth which have made this one of the stately pleasure grounds of England. However, the pleasurama complex has not obliterated the more aesthetic qualities of Beaulieu 'the beautiful place' and has certainly helped to take a lot of pressure off the woodlands. Nearby is Beaulieu Rails, which had its growth as a squatters' village when illegal occupiers of the forest had their homes demolished in one of the many forest clearances. On the open land of Beaulieu Heath and Beaulieu Hilltop will be found more than fifty barrows, most of which are thought to date from the Bronze Age. At that time it seems quite likely that the Solent may have been a fertile valley not yet drowned by the sea and the heathlands were probably at a greater height above sea level than they now are. In the late 1880s when excavations were taking place to provide new docks at Southampton, there was found embedded in peat some twenty feet below the surface of the low-tide mud the remains of red-deer, wild cattle, reindeer and of varieties of boar, horse and hare. A hammer stone and a bone needle were also found. The last of England's great lost places lies beneath the waters of the Solent.

Bucklet's Hard is now a popular yachtsman's haven. Most of the famous men-of-war built here were constructed under the direction of members of the local Adams family. Today the two rows of red brick cottages that form the main street of the village are the only memorials of the great days of sail and wooden walls. The place however, has an evocative magic all its own. On the south coast I think it can only be matched by the mysterious, rather forlorn atmosphere of Bosham – where Canute attempted to hold back the waves. Due to the crowds of summer visitors, however, in both cases it is an atmosphere that nowadays can only really be captured out of season in the months of late autumn or early spring. It may be a personal failing but I have no real liking for the sea in winter. But, at all events, visions of Nelson and Hood are hard to conjur up here in summer when the past glories of red, white and blue seem reflected only in the shorts of sunburnt children who, with the additions of yellows, greens and the more garish complexities of the dye-makers pallet, scutter around the quayside like so many tremulous butterflies.

Strictly speaking Lymington stands outside the area of the New Forest proper. There is a lot of new building here – for the Hampshire planners seem to have given up the ghost as far as consent and control are concerned on the seaboard west of the forest. Lymington is now virtually continuous with Milford and Milford similarly with Christchurch. Lymington is mostly to be discovered in its long main street – which incorporates building from the seventeenth to the twentieth centuries – climbing from the waterside toward its massively cupolaed church which it bends around to peter out toward the western extremities of the town. The church is a medieval building largely rebuilt in the eighteenth century and provides an eye-catching centre-piece for the street.

The church at Milford-on-Sea is also medieval with considerable traces of Norman work. The old village has been greatly expanded by modern developments. Nearby, at the end of a long promontary stretching out into the Solent, is Hurst Castle. This was one of the coastal defences built by Henry VIII who, at different times, thought England was likely to be invaded by either the French or the Spaniards. It once housed Charles I, brought here from the fortress of Carisbrooke and destined ultimately to travel to London and execution.

Moving northward we return to the true forest at Boldre which has a church whose origins date from the time of the Conqueror himself. William Gilpin, the early topographer and historian, was vicar here from 1771 to 1804 and lies buried in the churchyard. The church stands in isolation from the village, which is rather scattered though tending to concentrate in the valley of the River Bolder which is spanned at Boldre by a five arched bridge.

Before leaving this southern area entirely it should perhaps be mentioned that not far from the west bank of the Beaulieu estuary is Sowley Pond which was once the site of the only iron-works in the immediate neighbourhood of the New Forest. The works closed down early in the nineteenth century. Some of the iron-stone used came from the local cliffs and local people often gathered it at the foreshore and carried it to the works. Some of the fuel used obviously came from the forest. But, when restrictions began to be imposed on the uses to which forest timber could be put, the works, lying far from a coal supply, went the way of its Wealden brethren.

Ringwood is the traditional capital of the northern area of

the forest, though, in fact it lies a little outside the forest boundary. The place has seen much modern building and its church was rebuilt in the last century. It was from Ringwood that James, Duke of Monmouth, in flight after his disastrous defeat at Sedgemoor wrote to James II imploring that he be pardoned for his rebellion. The letter cut no ice with the frosty monarch and Monmouth ultimately faced his death bravely enough.

Monmouth's rebellion did not greatly touch Hampshire. Many of Monmouth's Protestant adherents came from the neighbouring counties of Dorset and Wiltshire, though the bulk of course, came from Somerset. But the last act of Monmouth's own personal tragedy was played out in the New Forest. He was finally to be captured on Horton Common not far from Ringwood. But some of his adherents escaped and two of them, Nelthorpe and Hicks, sought refuge at the home of Dame Alicia Lisle at Moyles Court some seven miles from Fordingbridge. Dame Alicia was a widow of seventy, her Roundhead husband having been assassinated in Switzerland in 1664. She and her son however, were Royalists, and so we have the familiar spectacle of the English Civil War, a house divided against itself. But Dame Alicia was a Protestant Royalist and perhaps considered that she owed a duty to Monmouth's men in offering them shelter from the pursuit of James' II's troops. But the shelter was hardly safe. The men were discovered and Dame Alicia found herself hauled off to Winchester to stand trial before the dreaded Judge Jefferies.

At first the jury had the courage to enter a finding of not guilty – but then, perhaps intimidated by Jefferies, changed their minds and condemned her. Jefferies now pronounced that the old lady should be burnt at the stake. Even James II thought this was going too far and "of his clemency" decided that she should be beheaded instead. So Dame Alicia was duly taken to the Square at Winchester and beheaded on 2nd September 1685. It was one of Jefferies's most bloody acts and brought the reign of terror echoing from the villages of Somerset and Wiltshire into this quiet, secluded area of the forest. Jefferies judicial murders of men and boys – most of them illiterate – who carried pitchforks and billhooks for the dashing Duke was surpassed in this savage sentence carried out on an old woman who had done no more than offer temporary refuge to two panic-stricken latter day Cavaliers.

In the far north of the forest stands the hill known as Bramshaw Telegraph which is marked by a belt of Scots pine. The hill is just over four hundred feet above sea-level and was once topped by a semaphore station, one of chain of such stations which linked London to Plymouth and Portsmouth. The station was manned by an officer and two men – one of whom was alternate look-out. After 1816 the semaphore used was a mast with two arms, invented by Sir Home Popham, and continued in use until 1847. The original semaphore system was a French invention and seems to have been introduced into England around 1795. Ten stations maintained communication between Portsmouth and London and it is said that the one on Southsea Common had enough work to keep it on the go all day long. Greenwich-time, relayed by semaphore, was said to reach Portsmouth in forty-five seconds. There was a total of sixty-seven signals representing various letters, phrases and figures. But the great draw-back of the semaphore system was that it was only efficient in daytime and was because of this that the electric telegraph achieved its eventual triumph. Yet, at the time that the electric system was first being canvassed, it was maintained that the semaphore system had become so efficient that the electric system could not hope to compete.

One vestige of the semaphore system still remains. When we speak of a message being sent 'along the line' we do not use a phrase that originated with the electric system, but with the semaphore telegraph and its sytem of relaying. There are a large number of Telegraph Hills in England and almost all owe their names to the early semaphore station which once stood upon their summits. Not far from Bramshaw Telegraph is Brook, a small hamlet neighboured by Gibbet Wood, which is said to commemorate the fact that a gibbet once stood alongside the road here.

But perhaps the most famous site in the whole forest, which also has gruesome associations, is also to be found in this northern area, the Rufus Stone. The present stone dates from 1841 and was put up on the site of one that had become weathered and defaced but which was firmly believed to mark the site of the oak tree from which glanced the arrow which killed William Rufus. William was killed on 2nd August 1100 and the arrow, traditionally, is said to have been shot by Sir Walter Tyrell. Rufus was afterward taken to Winchester and was buried in the cathedral there. There have been many explanations of the event. It has been alleged that it was a murder of revenge, that it was the result of a clerical conspiracy, even that it could have been an accident. Believe what you will. The Rufus Stone is the appropriate place to come to ruminate upon the possibilities.

Contemplation of Rufus's violent end at the intervention of an oak tree seems an appropriate place to leave the New Forest and to consider what could loosely be termed its surrounding woodland. Away to the west lies Dorset's remaining major tract of woodland, Cranborne Chase, where deer are still stalked in traditional manner. But the days when venison pasty was once the regular fare of the local people are long past. The deer is no longer plentiful here and the local poacher is little more than a memory in myth and folk song. This is Hardy Country – and parts of Cranborne Chase could still transport the novelist to the elemental world of his beloved Wessex. Nearby is Shaftesbury and that Georgian masterpiece, Blandford Forum. Shaftesbury has its ruins and public school to entice the visitor while Blandford Forum is renowned for its many architectural gems.

Across the waters of the Solent, but still in Hampshire, lies the Isle of Wight and its Forest of Avington. This is now a working forest and lies on the north side of the island a little inland from the yachting capital of Cowes. It is visited by a considerable number of holidaymakers and all the resorts of the island are within easy reach, though none have much bearing on the history or present day organisation of Avington.

The Alice Holt Forest – to the east of the New Forest and lying close to the Surrey border – has largely lost any trace of the wildness that it once possessed. It is now a leading example of planned, economic silviculture. There is, however, a nature reserve and a heronry and nearby at Alton, is a museum with an interesting natural-history collection. The forest covers in the region of two thousand acres and the former Ranger's Lodge is now used by the Forestry Commission as a research centre. In fact Alice Holt Forest is just the place for children old enough to have acquired more than a passing interest in woodlands and ecology in general for here it is most obvious that man is now attempting to work with, rather than against, nature. The work may smack a little of landscape gardening – but it is at least a valid compromise.

Alton stands on the edge of Alice Holt and is a market-town with a number of Georgian houses in its main street. The parish church dates from the time of the Conquest. The town is also a long-standing centre of the brewing industry and was mentioned for the quality of its ale in Thackeray's *Vanity Fair*. Today the air is often tinged with the pungent aroma of hops and barley and both Watney Mann and Harp Lager have breweries in the town. Nearby the village of Bentley has close links with the Scout and Guide Associations for it was once home to the Baden-Powells.

Bere Forest – or, as the Forestry Commission purists will have it, the Forest of Bere – spills across the Hampshire boundary into Sussex and is now just over 3,000 acres in extent – though not all this is one continuous tract. There is, as has already been mentioned, some danger that the Forest of Bere will one day come to be incorporated into a metropolitan region based upon nearby Portsmouth, maybe as part of an amenity area, maybe to be completely disafforested before being covered by new development. However, the Forestry Commission maintains that this woodland forms an important part of England's timber reserves and the forest will certainly not go without a fight. Yet, if it is to be saved from further threats, it will be mainly because of the efforts of local people.

At the northern fringe of Bere Forest stands Corhampton with a fine Saxon church some of which, though not very much, has been rebuilt. Not far away lies Droxford with a Norman church, a seventeenth-century manor house and an eighteenth-century rectory. It was at Droxford's now disused railway station that the main figures involved with the launching of the D-Day invasion of 1944 waited during those fateful hours while the weather changed to make possible the momentous events of 5th June. The remains of pill-boxes and artillery sites in this region still provide rather more concrete reminders of those days.

To the east lies the Weald – once probably the most densely afforested region in England. Today there survives Ashdown Forest and St Leonard's Forest as reminders of the vanished Andresweald of Saxon days, together with many small knots of woodland. To the north, on Berkshire's furthest fringe, are the woodlands of Windsor Great Park and Windsor Forest – all that remains of the Wealden woods in the immediate neighbourhood of London. St Leonard's Forest is neighboured by Horsham and East Grinstead is not far from the boundaries of Ashdown. Neither can be described as particularly prepossessing places. The Wealden villages are noted for their charm and have attracted large numbers of commuter and retired settlers. Over the past thirty years this settlement has been so intense as to alter drastically the character of many villages. New developments in the Weald are now strictly limited even to the extent that, in Surrey at least, it is becoming increasingly rare for planning permission to be given for extensions to old properties. This attempt to preserve Wealden charm must be said to be rather belated.

North-east of London, Epping and Hainault Forests have Chingford as their real centre for here is a museum which, like that at Hampshire's Alton, has a considerable part of its collection devoted to local studies. In fact this seems to be the only real justification for the existence of local museums. Those that try, with a scattered collection of exhibits which attempts to cover everything from the Bronze Age to the clothes worn by our Edwardian great-aunts, to ape their bigger city brothers are, in all but the rarest of cases, simply trying to achieve the impossible. Usually such collections fail to attract the visitor who can find a much more comprehensive display in his native city. Yet the visitor is often inordinately interested in the locality he has come to visit and a collection which deals with local history, local personalities and the particular geology, vegetation and industry of the region will do much more to awaken his interest. Many local museums have already moved in this direction and have really become virtual field-study centres. In fact museum is really an inappropriate title for these centres.

Moving northward to the central Midlands the major forest areas are to be found in Cannock Chase and Charnwood Forest. Cannock is very much made up of conifer plantations, indeed it is basically a mixture of heathland and conifer. Its nearest large town is the cathedral city of Lichfield, renowned as the boyhood home of Dr Samuel Johnson and for its many tea-shops. There are other wooded areas, of course, especially in Northamptonshire, North Warwickshire and in the remnants of Arden. Come to that, even Birmingham possesses its own woodland in the largely conifer plantations of the Lickey Hills. In north Oxfordshire is the Forest of Wychwood, though this is in private hands and access to the public is extremely limited, though nearby Woodstock is well worth a visit as is Blenheim Palace, home of the Dukes of Marlborough and with its many Churchillian associations.

Yet of these central Midland forests it is Cannock and Charnwood which draw most visitors. Cannock is roughly divided in use between a leisure area, with its pony-trekking and so forth and economic forestry. Charwood has Leicester as its nearest large town, with its de Montfort associations and a hosiery and knitware industry which also spills over into such neighbouring towns as Hinkley and Market Bosworth. There is also Loughborough, once known for its conglomeration of colleges which are now a university in their own right and, for those interested in the romantic aspect of our history, the Field of Bosowrth, and the tragedy that led to the fall of the Yorkists and the initiation of the Tudor monarchy.

North from Charnwood there is Sherwood Forest and still further the woodlands of the Derbyshire dales. Sherwood is now a roughly equal mixture of conifer and deciduous woodland. It has, of course, its Robin Hood's Oak and various other places accredited with some association with the famous outlaw and his men. But there is also Newstead Abbey, the ancestral home of Lord Byron while a little northward lie the Dukeries – most nowadays, like Welbeck, no longer in the hands of the ennobled. South is Nottingham, the self-styled 'Queen of the Midlands', a modern university town, and the home of Boots the Chemist, and Player's cigarettes. On a more historical note it has its castle, with its tales of King John and the Sheriff, and the time-honoured pub 'The Trip to Jerusalem' cut from the rock beneath Castle Hill.

Eastward into East Anglia we find a strange area that traditionally was not forest at all though it is now certainly a very afforested place. This is Breckland, that peculiar rise in the land that straddles the Norfolk-Suffolk borderland and which centres upon the market-town of Thetford. It is a Forestry-Commission plantation almost exclusively devoted to conifers. As would be expected in East Anglia, particularly in a region which has for long proved unsuitable for most forms of agriculture, it is particularly rich in wildlife. There is a heronry at Livermere and gulls roost on Thompson Water some fifteen miles north east of Thetford. There are four Breckland sites in the control of the Nature Conservancy and two large sites are controlled by County Naturalists Trusts, the Norfolk one covering Lang Mere and nearby Wrentham Heath, the Suffolk one being on Thetford Heath. To the south of Breckland is Bury St Edmunds with its ruined medieval Abbey and memories of the days when the town was an out-of-town pleasure resort for the Elizabethan nobility. Bury St Edmunds did not, in fact, begin to lose this reputation for courtly gaiety until the rise of the spa towns of Tunbridge Wells and Bath in the late seventeenth century.

North into Yorkshire we find the Rye Dale Woods lying some ten miles from Thirsk on the Yorkshire Moors and, to the west of them, Fountains Abbey Woods, the only large remnant still surviving of the once extensive Forest of Knaresborough. Fountains Abbey draws more visitors than the woods themselves and nearby is Knaresborough, a bustling market-town, home of Mother Shipton and the famous petrifying well. Not far away is the spa town of Harrogate – now more updated from its past glories to be a leading conference centre.

The largest area of woodland in the North-West is Hardknott Forest, a Forestry Commission holding almost exclusively devoted to the conifer and standing within the Lake District National Park. There are a number of other, deciduous woodlands to be found on the fringes of the Lake

District, mostly in the northern area such as Barrow Wood near Keswick. However, it is fairly obvious that the woodlands here are far from being the major attraction to the visitor, though they certainly help to enhance the splendour of the Lake District scenery.

Moving to the western Midlands the two largest areas of woodland are both to be found in Shropshire, at Wenlock Edge and at the Forest of Wyre which also occupies part of Worcestershire as well. Added to this the county has considerable woodland in the Ludlow region – mostly scattered and unified in name only under the title of Mortimer Forest – as well as the remnants of the Forest of Clun. Wenlock Edge is very largely deciduous and draws its visitors not so much for the woodland as for the extensive views it offers over the Shropshire Plain. Nearby Much Wenlock is an ancient town with a ruined priory, associations with the border novelist Mary Webb and a revived Charter Day Fayre. Nearby, also, are the ruins of Buildwas Abbey, the original Iron Bridge across the Severn and the fortress-like Wilderhope Manor.

The Forest of Wyre is some 6,000 acres in extent and includes in this the Forest of Rock and other woodlands in North Worcestershire. The nearby town here is Bewdley, once a thriving eighteenth-century river-port on the Severn, which retains many of its Georgian buildings. It was the birthplace of Stanley Baldwin and once, briefly the headquarters of General Charles de Gaulle and the Free French Army. Not far away is the village of Cleobury Mortimer whose church has a twisted spire and which manages to hold an artistic festival each year. Wyre is one of those forest areas which is presently receiving close scrutiny by the Forestry Commission in the light of its increasing attraction to visitors.

Southward we again return to the fringes of the Forest of Dean – though here I feel we should take a trip across the border into Gwent to mention what are known collectively as the Wye Valley Woodlands. These include the Forest of Tintern – so beloved by Wordsworth and Kilvert – and, of course, the ruins of Tintern Abbey. There were once great ironworks here.

This circuit of the forestlands has of necessity been rather brief. Some small areas have been omitted. Nevertheless, I hope it will indicate that the forests are more than trees and history and that they are worth visiting not only for themselves but for the joys of the rest of the countryside in which they are to be found.

10

The Wildlife Story

There are two simple sides to England's wildlife story – namely, what we have already lost and what we have left – or, in respect of the latter, what we have still to lose. We have already lost a great number of species. To discuss England's wildlife properly it is necessary that, in some respects, this be both an historical appreciation and a contemporary analysis. But it is possible to take historical appreciation too far and it would be pointless to bemoan the fact that no one bothered to preserve the dinosaur and his clutch of over-mighty subjects.

If we extend our terms of reference beyond the Anglo-Saxon and Roman period we will discover that once not only was most of lowland Britain covered in woodland, but that most of the highland chalk areas were as well. These were long ago cleared by Neolithic man, not with stone axes, but simply by fire. It would have been useless for these early settlers to attempt to clear the dense oak woodlands of the lowland areas by the same means simply because they were too wet, large tracts being almost swamp. But the chalk areas were a different matter. Here the soil was dry and well drained and it was an easy matter to burn off the woodland cover.

Neolithic man's activities do not seem to have been particularly harmful to any of the native animal population – with the one notable exception of the giant 'Irish' elk. This animal was really a large fallow deer with enormous antlers and vaguely related to the present-day North-American moose. It has been dubbed the 'Irish' elk largely because most of the preserved skeletal remains of the animal have been discovered in Irish peat bogs. It was rather a docile creature and Neolithic man must have regarded it as a most convenient form of meat supply. It is certain that Neolithic man, and his

Bronze-Age successors drove the 'Irish' elk well on the way to extinction.

Bronze-Age man added to the number of animal species in the country. From the Continent he introduced the horse and dog and he added to the number of sheep, goats, pigs and cattle that had formed the basis of Neolithic herds. The reindeer had already begun to move northward, but apart from the 'Irish' elk, Bronze-Age man would have faced the same animals as had his Neolithic predecessors – namely the bear, lynx, wolf, wild-cat, wild-boar, badger, fox otter, elk and the red deer. Our Bronze-Age ancestors also cleared some of the higher lowland areas, not because population was expanding, but because there came about a climatic change in which the weather became drier and the chalk uplands dried out to such an extent that they became suitable only for grazing.

When the Iron-Age Celts first arrived at about B.C. 600, they added little to the native animal species apart from improving the breed of cattle and pigs, the importation of a new type of horse – which has been thought to have resembled the Exmoor pony – and the introduction of a new breed of dog, the mastiff, which the Romans were to dub *pugnaces molossi* and to send to Rome in great numbers for the gladiatorial arena.

There must also have been numerous species of bird. But here the evidence is very scanty. The range of British birds does not begin to become clear until the Anglo-Saxon period. Then we have to rely very largely on gleanings from Anglo-Saxon literature and, because much of this was cast in the epic mould, there is a marked preoccupation with birds of prey.

The Romans were responsible for the introduction of one major animal into England, namely the fallow deer. They have also been credited with the introduction of the pheasant and the domestic chicken – though here the evidence is less certain. On the debit side they pushed back the area of habitation for the lynx, brown bear and the aurochs – or European bison – though all three must have considerably re-established themselves in the lowland region after the Roman withdrawal. The wolf certainly increased in numbers at this time.

With the exception of the fallow deer the native animal species of England showed no marked alteration between Roman and Saxon times – and the Saxons were not destined to introduce any new species. Saxon settlement was to have the effect of driving the brown bear to extinction, though it was not to disappear from northern England until the late tenth century. Though it is not a certainty, the lynx probably survived in the north of England until the early years of the Norman Conquest. Wolves and foxes were such a menace that King Edgar seems to have employed a professional wolf hunter. The number of wolves in Saxon England was greatly reduced in the course of time – but there were still large numbers surviving at the time of the Norman invasion.

But the Saxons did know three birds which cannot now, by any stretch of the ornithological imagination, be described as English residents. All were birds of prey: the eagle owl, being the largest European owl and now nesting largely in Norway and Spain; the gyr-falcon is today known as the Greenland or Iceland falcon, both species nesting in Iceland and the Iceland falcon as far south as the Faeroe Islands. Both these birds are now only the most rare of winter visitors. But the Saxons also recorded the presence in England of the vulture – the griffon vulture which now nests no nearer than Spain. The surname Griffin has been said to derive from the occupation of men charged with hunting down this bird, or to have been given as a nickname to those who were of a mercenary or venal nature.

Together with what may yet be proved to be the far from mythical unicorn the griffin has long been a favourite heraldic device – though here the griffon vulture has been transformed into a cross between an eagle and a lion. The griffon vulture ceased to be an English resident well before the close of the Middle Ages. It continued to return as an occasional winter visitor but, since 1843, it is on record as having turned up only three times on the English coast. Its disappearance may, of course, be tied up with the fact that, in general after the close of the Middle Ages, England became a very much cleaner place to live.

Mention of bird life leads us to a consideration of the native English tree, the number of species of which were not to be augmented until the development of economic forestry toward the middle of the nineteenth century. England's present-day forests and the plantations within them fall into two basic categories, deciduous trees, which cast their leaves in winter and which are generally broad-leaved, and conifer evergreens. Despite popular opinion to the contrary the conifer has always played some part in the English forest story, not only in such northern forests as Delamere, but more generally via the yew. The yew grows in almost all English forests and, apart from its association with ancient religious cults, was especially regarded in medieval times as the source of the timber for England's longbows.

Like the yew the oak once had religious associations and, according to Pliny, Druidical ceremonies were once enacted in sacred groves of oak trees. There are two species of oak native to England, namely the common oak and the durmast oak, while there exist at least three other varieties introduced from abroad. It is the oak which still provides the essential character of many of the older forest areas, such as Dean and Sherwood, and this is very largely because of the government's preoccupation with oakwood as naval timber which was to persist until the mid nineteenth century. Their acorn fruit was largely responsibly for calling into existence the medieval common right of pannage.

Of other more common English trees the ash has also been connected with ancient religions. But here the connection has not been as well established as in the case of the oak and yew. It produces a seed shaped like a small nut and which is winged to aid dispersal.

The sycamore also produces winged seeds, two wings as against the ash's one, which small children seem to have taken to calling helicopters. Although originally introduced from southern Europe it is now general throughout England and has some claim to be regarded as the English teak for its timber is very strong. It is increasingly used in furniture making.

Common enough to be termed a 'weed' in some counties the English elm is said to have been introduced to this country by the Romans. It has to be said there is no evidence to support the claim. It is mainly to be found in hedgerows rather than in forests, though the landscape gardeners of the eighteenth century made considerable use of it in parklands. It is a rather treacherous tree, sometimes casting a branch without warning. This can be a rather unpleasant characteristic for a tree which lines so many of our lanes. The ravages of Dutch-elm disease have shown up just how many areas of the countryside, especially the Midland counties, have, up to now, preserved their wooded appearance very largely because of the presence of the elm.

Of trees of somewhat smaller stature than these the alder is confined to moist woodland and boggy ground while the silver birch is common all over England, but most common in the south. The beech also is more general in the south of England and thrives on chalky soils. It has a considerable commercial value. The copper beech, with distinctive red-brown leaves, is an ornamental variety often cultivated for garden hedgerows.

The horse chestnut, whose blossom once moved Housman to write one of his best known poems "When the Chestnut Casts its Flambeaux", is not an English native but was originally introduced from Greece. However, it has long been widespread and 'sticky buds' and conkers form part of the lore of almost every English child. Its major use was to provide shade for cattle rather than to meet the needs of forestry.

Of the conifers the yew and the Scots pine are native to England, the scots pine being indigenous to the north of England as well as to Scotland. A large number of conifer species – including the Chile pine or monkey puzzle – have been introduced for ornamental purposes and are largely confined to parks and gardens. Most of the remainder have been introduced in connection with economic forestry, including the Norway spruce with its enormous cylindrical cones and the European larch whose cones are small and ovoid in shape. From North America comes the giant douglas fir and the scarcely smaller giant fir itself. The douglas fir is especially cultivated on some of the Forestry Commission holdings, particularly in the plantations of the north of England. Smaller than these is the white spruce, also introduced from North America. Its cones are the same shape as those of the douglas fir, but only half their size. This species has been widely planted in the south of England.

Of course, this by no means pretends to be an exhaustive

list of the trees growing in England. There are a large number of specialist books dealing with the subject – which anyone with a particular interest in arboriculture would be advised to consult. Of the elder, holly, hazel, willow and many others I have said nothing here. But I have confined myself largely to mentioning those trees which are either most common in our woodlands and hedgerows or which are now cultivated mainly for their importance to modern forestry.

Economic forestry was a term yet to be thought of when the Normans first brought in the rabbit and the rat – the latter probably first entering England from the Continent in the twelfth century. The rabbit, in all probability, did not turn up until much later – it has been suggested in the reign of King John (1199-1216). Before this 'rights of warren' do not make mention of rabbits, although they included the hare which, by then, had been in England for at least a thousand years. The Norman sportsmen can have had no idea of just how drastically the rabbit was to affect the English countryside.

From the twelfth century also dates the first record of the beaver in Britain, noted by the Bishop of Brecon, Gerald Cambrensis. Gerald saw the beaver in West Wales and at the time he was writing it had almost certainly disappeared from England, though there is no reason to suppose that it had not been present earlier. But, as it is not mentioned in either the Doomsday Book or in any surviving Anglo Saxon literature, it seems reasonable to assume that it died out in most parts of England either before or during the Roman occupation.

During the later Middle Ages, as England became increasingly disafforested the number of animal and bird species became progressively threatened. But some birds, at least, were to be offered a measure of legislative protection. An Act of 1534 gave protection to certain birds and their eggs between 31st May and 1st August. Included in the species covered by this measure were the crane, heron, spoonbill, bittern and the great bustard. Unlike the others the great bustard had been a resident for less than a century, but its size made it an attractive meal for the English peasant and there must have been considerable danger that the new arrival would be eaten out of existence. Protection was also given to the kite, highly valued as a scavenger which cleared much of the offal from the town streets and middens. London's kites were numbered in thousands and their presence certainly helped to check the spread of epidemic disease.

But some of the birds on this early protection list seem to have sensed that only disaster awaited them if they remained in England. The spoonbill seems to have forsaken England of its own accord and is last reported as breeding in Suffolk in 1667. Just under a decade later comes the last report of the crane breeding in England – though, for many decades it continued to visit the East-Anglican fenlands. As in the case of the spoonbill there had been no change in its natural habitat – the first modern attempts to drain the fens had yet to come – and it would seem that it left England due to an inexplicable change in breeding habits. But seventeenth-century reclamation work in the fenland – and similar work in other centuries, especially the nineteenth – was to result in the extinction as breeding species of a large number of marsh-birds. These were to include the avocet, bittern, marsh-harrier, ruff, black-tailed godwit and Savi's warbler.

Just when the wolf disappeared as an English animal cannot be said with certainty, but it is likely that it was extinct even in the north by the end of the sixteenth century. The wild boar was still being hunted in Elizabethan times and James I is known to have hunted the boar in the Midlands. Shortly after this, it appears to have died out in the south, though it probably lingered a little longer on the Scottish border. Charles I made an attempt to import wild boar from France into the New Forest and as late as 1702 General Howe attempted to reintroduce the wild boar into Woolmer Forest. Of England's larger animals only the red deer lived in anything approaching safety, protected by the operation of the Forest Laws.

Up to this point one element which was to have a dire effect on wildlife in general – but particularly upon the bird population – was absent from the English scene. In general the larger animals had been eased out of their habitat and ultimately hunted to extinction. Except in the fenlands man had not made serious inroads into the bird populaton. These he did hunt, but largely with either the longbow or the crossbow. What drastically tipped the balance against the birds was first the introduction and later the improvement of the sporting-gun.

At first it was very expensive and dangerous to own a sporting gun. Even as late as the mid eighteenth century the poorer countryfolk continued to use the cross-bow. By the 1780s game-birds were being shot by the best shots of the day (using muzzle-loaders) at the rate of up to fifty per day. With the introduction of the breech-loader and a more organized approach to the sport this average could shoot up to around a thousand birds a day for a good shot. England stood in danger of being emptied of its birds.

The great difference in the size of an average day's haul between, let us say, 1800 and 1870, was due to a combination of factors. The introduction of the breech-loader took the walking out of shooting, for it now became the practice for game-shooters to employ a loader who charged one gun while they were busy discharging the other. The second most important change was in the increasing organization of the sport, the construction of hides and the practice of employing beaters to drive the birds towards where the sportsmen were waiting. By the 1780s game shooting had become a static business – at least for those with guns in their hands – and it was far easier to shoot birds driven forwards in flocks than to pick off individual ones amidst woodland.

It may be just as well to mention at this point that shooting-men were often on bad terms with the fox-hunting fraternity. The hunters tended to protect areas of woodland as covert for the fox whilst the rural gunmen protected other similar areas as essential breeding grounds for the game-birds. The fox, of course, was quite unable to differentiate between the two and would often lead the pursuing hounds into a game preserve rather than a fox covert. The natural result was disturbed birds, and often a breeding ground rendered useless for the rest of the season. It was from the shooting man rather than from the average farmer that the fox-hunters often had to face their greatest opposition.

Pheasants were introduced into England in the late eighteenth century, but did not begin to become at all numerous as a game species until the middle of the nineteenth. After this their population seems to have exploded due to the care of the gamekeepers and it became commonplace for bags of 1,000 a day to be taken during the season and figures in excess of 2,000 were by no means uncommon. The Victorians believed not so much in shooting as in massacre.

This preoccupation with the game-preserves on the part of the landowners was certainly not without far-reaching effects on English wildlife in general. It was the job of the gamekeeper to keep the preserves well-stocked. This he did not only by keeping out poachers and, where possible, foxes, but also by waging war on almost every creature that would seem to offer some threat to the birds – whether that threat were real or not. The woodlands became infested with traps and within the space of no more than three decades three more of England's animal species, the pole-cat, pine marten and the wild-cat, had been driven into the inaccessible regions of Wales and Scotland.

The gamekeepers also engaged in a shooting war against birds of prey. Anything that looked vaguely like a hawk was to be shot from the skies. One casualty was to be the honey-buzzard which, although a member of the hawk family, was perfectly harmless to game-birds. At the beginning of the nineteenth century this bird was common all over the south of England. By 1885 only a couple of pairs were known to exist in the whole country, these nesting in the New Forest. Another visitor, the marsh-harrier, had wisely decided, by the turn of the century, to make its trips to England very occasional indeed. Of resident birds the kite, hen-harrier, raven and common buzzard suffered severely. The kite, which we have already seen being put on a protected list as early as the sixteenth century, was common to almost all English counties at the beginning of the nineteenth century. Well before the dawn of the twentieth it had been completely banished from England and survived only in Wales – and there in very small numbers. The hen-harrier – an upland bird – was exterminated as an English resident and only managed to maintain a toe-hold as a British resident in the far north of Scotland. By 1900 the raven and common buzzard survived in any numbers only along the Welsh Border. From the viewpoint of the gamekeeper and his employer the job had been well done – the barbed wire fences lined with stoats, weasels and their brethren bore eloquent testimony to that.

Yet the gamekeepers had done their job far too well. With large-scale tooth and claw virtually removed from the woodlands the smaller creatures now flourished relatively unchecked and were to cause far more damage to the game-bird population than ever had been done by their slaughtered enemies. The population of rabbits, wood-pigeons, grey squirrels and rats multiplied alarmingly. The rat in particular was soon to be found decimating many a preserve.

But it was not only the game-keeper who was responsible for the decline of what remained of the native bird and animal life in nineteenth century England. The fox and the game-birds survived largely because it was the policy of the landed gentry to protect them – even after the ritual slaughter there were always some left. Some native animals continued to fend fairly well for themselves, including the badger and the hare and, to a lesser extent, the otter. But the birds were threatened not only by the gamekeepers' guns but by the activities of the professional egg-collector. (Animals were also collected and there was a Victorian boom in the trade of the taxidermist.)

In general it was only when a bird began to become rare that the egg-collectors became interested – the gamekeeper having brought some wildbird species to the point of extinction, the activities of the professional egg-collectors threatened to complete the process. The great bustard was exterminated by shooting but the white-tailed eagle and the osprey suffered greatly at the hands of the egg-collectors. The golden eagle, like the white-tailed eagle, was also badly affected by shooting for it was believed that both preyed on sheep, and the Commissioners of Supply offered a reward of three shilling for every one killed. The golden eagle would seem to be one bird that has always been confined to upland areas and, even before the Commissioners of Supply began their sponsored onslaught, it was largely to be found in Scotland and some parts of Wales. But the white-tailed eagle was far more widespread, being found as far south as Hampshire and the Isle of Wight. By 1835 however, when the Commissioners withdrew their reward, it was no longer an English bird. Indeed, it hardly survived even as a British bird for it had disappeared even from the Scottish mainland and was to be found only in the scattered Outer Isles. The golden eagle had been confined to its present-day habitat, the far north of Scotland.

Yet this was also a time of new introductions to the English wildlife scene – some accidental, some premeditated. If we were losing some of our oldest natural species we were at least to gain some rather eccentric replacements. To embellish their estates landowners were to introduce the muntjac, the Japanese sika deer and the Chinese water-deer. All three were destined to escape from parklands in various parts of the country and to establish themselves in the wild. Wallabys were later to become established on the Staffordshire-Derbyshire border on the moorland in the neighbourhood of Leek, and have now become something of a tourist attraction in their own right. In recent years a number of animals have escaped from what are euphemistically termed 'fur farms'. These include the mink and the coypu. Campaigns have been mounted to limit the spread of these as both are extremely destructive, but both have had only limited success. The musk-rat, another escapee, does seem to have been stamped out. The same can hardly be said of the grey squirrel which was introduced as a picturesque addition to our countryside in 1876. It would seem that the grey squirrel was originally introduced even earlier than this when a colony was established in Montgomeryshire. But this Welsh version appears to have died out. The grey-squirrel was soon found bearing the appelation of the tree-rat, for it preyed upon the eggs of game and other birds just as did the rat with the added facility of being able to clamber through the trees. This unpleasant fact apart, it was soon to be engaged in ceaseless warfare with the native red squirrel. As it was a larger, and altogether more vicious animal than the herbivorous red, it naturally drove the older resident out of large areas of the countryside. Its spread was quite rapid and, before the end of the 1930s, the red squirrel had been evicted from most of England, lingering very largely in the north and especially in the region of the Lake District. Today there are only two colonies of red squirrels in the south of England, one in the New Forest and the other on Dorset's Brownsea Island.

A number of species of bird were also introduced over this period, again largely by landowners who wished to add to the variety of their sport. As early as the late eighteenth century Suffolk saw the introduction of the red-legged partridge. In more recent years this has been joined by the American bobwhite quail – again introduced by the sporting fraternity. Other recent additions have been largely accidental and include the Carolina duck, ruddy duck, Canada goose and the manadarin duck. Given favourable conditions there is no reason why these species should not multiply. On another track, the chipmunks liberated not so long ago in Cheshire may yet multiply exceedingly – and there seems every possibility that this Disneyland creature will become just as great a pest as the ubiquitous grey squirrel.

Selective breeding and importation was also to lead to an increase in the number of species of English domestic animals, both of the pet variety and in connection with husbandry. Two species of domestic animal should perhaps, be mentioned. Of these one, the Highland cattle, should not really be termed domestic at all, for it is the lineal descendant of our native wild cattle. The other is no longer an English resident, but once was and has recently been reintroduced into northern Scotland. This is the reindeer which, we have already seen, was once common in southern England.

In recent years a number of attempts have been made to reintroduce some of England's vanished species – especially birds. Many are so far confined to Scotland, such as the white-tailed eagle which has recently been reintroduced on Fir Isle, and the osprey which, since the mid 1950s, has re-established itself on a small scale on Speyside.

We have thus arrived at the point of considering what remains of England's once teeming wild-life. With this is associated contemporary efforts to protect and foster what we have left and also to re-establish some species once native but now no longer so. A few of the vanished species do exist in England, but only in zoos, as is the case with the lynx and wolf which have been imported from Europe where a few still survive in the wild. There is a case to be made for the creation of a wildlife park in Britain which could contain animals once native to these Islands. It does seem rather ridiculous that we now have so many safari parks devoted to the animals of other continents while there exists nowhere in Britain a wildlife park concentrating upon European species almost all of whom were once native to Britain.

On the small scale many individual efforts have been made to preserve existing wildlife. One movement is that of the small nature reserve, sometimes a private venture, sometimes supported by such institutions as universities or country trusts, sometimes controlled by the Nature Conservancy. A large number of these are in woodland areas and many have as their preoccupation the preservation of just one species. In Devon one reserve is devoted to the doormouse and another in neighbouring Somerset exists to preserve the habitat of the badger. Locally neither species can be said to be faced with extinction, although nationally their numbers have been steadily declining over the past century. Both however, need an environment which is scarcely that most favoured by modern agricultural methods and the creation of such reserves is one way of ensuring that their numbers do not fall to danger level.

Even in this pinched and tight-belted age a large number of privately owned parklands still maintain their herds of fallow deer. But the red deer has largely gone the way of most surviving former English species – north to Scotland. There are some fallow deer to be found in the Forest of Dean – though, perhaps it should be said not in the Forest of Dean proper, but in the woodlands of the western bank of the Wye from where they make occasional forays into the forest. The Dean's own red and fallow deer were exterminated in 1850 when – by order of Parliament – the deer were removed from the forest. In this year 150 bucks and more than 300 does are said to have been killed and thus the forest's ancient connection with deer was terminated. It would have been at an end some forty years earlier if steps had not been taken to build up the number of deer from the ten that, due to the skill of local poachers, were said to be the only survivors. In the light of the activities of 1850 it can only be wondered why any attempt was made to revive the Forest-of-Dean deer at all. In the New Forest, of course, the deer, including a small herd of red, do survive, though perhaps rather outnumbered by the ponies.

But the woodlands, especially the deciduous kind, remain major redoubts of birdlife. The kite has not been seen in the Forest of Dean for over a century. Yet, if it were to re-establish itself outside its meagre mid-Welsh confines, the forest would be as good a place as any for it to make its reappearance in England. Two birds of prey do survive in the woodlands, namely the buzzard and the sparrowhawk. The buzzard in fact, is fairly common to most types of English countryside and is, at present, our most common bird of prey. The sparrowhawk is especially numerous in the New Forest and in the counties of the West. But in many other areas the sparrowhawk's numbers have fallen greatly since the large-scale introduction of agricultural chemicals. There are now some signs that its numbers are beginning to increase along the Welsh border and in the northern counties.

Of larger birds which do not belong to the hawk family the deciduous woodland is also home to the woodcock and turtle dove as well as to the distinctively plumaged jay. It is also home for a clutch of woodpeckers, the green woodpecker, lesser-spotted woodpecker, the wryneck and the greater-spotted woodpecker, the latter being the most common and now spread even to London's parks and gardens. The green woodpecker – or yaffle – is also increasing in numbers, especially in the north of England. On the other side of the scales the lesser-spotted woodpecker is far from common anywhere and the wryneck is in steep decline, now being limited to only a few parts of Kent and Surrey. In country areas it was once well-known as 'the cuckoo's mate' as it arrives in England at the end of March. Unfortunately it is one of the few birds that can reasonably be expected to become extinct as an English breeding species within the next decade. Other deciduous woodland birds include the nightingale, redstart, wood warbler, treecreeper, nuthatch, brambling, hawfinch, blackcap and the long-tailed tit.

Conifer woodland tends to be the home of the black grouse though, apart from occasional pairs on Exmoor and the Quantocks, they do not penetrate further south than Staffordshire. The conifer plantations also give shelter to the long-eared owl, though this bird will sometimes nest on dunes, heathland or marsh. It is less common in the South and

Midlands than it is in the North. Its 'ears' have nothing to do with hearing, being merely elongated head feathers. The conifer forest is also home to England's smallest bird, the goldcrest, which will occasionally nest in areas of mixed woodland. The spread of conifer plantations has also greatly assisted in increasing the numbers of a few specific species of bird, including the crested tit, lesser redpoll and siskin. The siskin, once confined almost entirely to the Scottish Highlands, is now to be found as far south as the New Forest.

Of course a number of English birds, such as the osprey and avocet, have been so drastically reduced in numbers that they can never again be re-established on a large scale. Changes in population and environment have so radically affected the countryside that their re-establishment in anything approaching their former numbers is now an impossibility.

With the possible exception of the rat such wholesale slaughter of species as was witnessed in the nineteenth century is unlikely to be seen in our own times. But it must be said that whilst most birds now enjoy a reasonably rigorous protection, continued hunting is threatening the existence of both the badger and the otter. In the case of the red squirrel it is not man, but the grey squirrel, which now threatens to drive it from England completely.

If the threat to nineteenth-century wildlife was largely to be found in the development of the breech-loader – which saw off not only English species but, as mounted heads in Victorian halls proudly declared, an enormous amount of wildlife in every corner of the empire – the threat is now the somewhat more subtle one posed by the increasing use of agricultural chemicals. It is for this reason that the woodlands, which make only minor use of the products of the chemical revolution, are to be so prized as wildlife sanctuaties. Even so, birds and animals which live in woodland areas are hardly immune from chemicals for often their food will come from areas beyond the woodland itself, this being especially so in the case of birds of prey.

It is rather ironic to consider that bird life has been fostered, especially in the north, by the control of industrial pollution only to be increasingly exposed to the newer chemical variety. In one form or another pesticides have been a severe check on

England's wildlife population. Some kill off insects directly, others starve them by killing off weeds and in both cases birds are robbed of a major portion of their diet. In other cases birds and animals eat seeds and insects which have been contaminated by chemical sprays. In Scotland the golden eagle suffered a severe check when sheep began to be dipped in a sheep-dip compound based on adrelin. As they were scavengers they picked up adrelin-contaminated flesh which was poisonous to them. Not until after this chemical was withdrawn did the golden eagle population begin to recover. It was not until dieldrin was partly withdrawn – in 1962 when it was agreed that it would be largely used in autumn and not in spring as had formerly been the case – that the fox population of East Anglia began to recover together with that of the English bird population in general. More than 1,000 foxes had been found dead in East Anglia in the winter of 1959/60 and bird deaths the following spring were numbered in thousand in almost every county.

The existence of Special Nature Reserves in forest areas, of the efforts of the Nature Conservancy, local County Naturalists' Trusts – which generally manage reserves of their own – and of other bodies may, taken together, produce the largest overall conservation policy of any nation in Europe. But their efforts are surrounded by a largely hostile environment. If it were not for the presence of humans it would no doubt be a much safer proposition for England's birds and animals to live in the towns rather than in the countryside. Agriculture long ago ceased to be a craft and became an industry. With this change came industrial pollution which, in many places, has convulsed and emptied the rivers and turned the land into a wildlife graveyard. Not until the agricultural chemical industry, the planners of our basically urban society and those with a scientific – rather than sentimental – appreciation of our natural wildlife get together to hammer out a nation-wide countryside policy can there be any real hope for our wildlife's future. The existence of a whole range of organizations and societies from the Royal Society for the Protection of Birds to the Nature Conservancy all, essentially, fighting skirmishes of their own rather than concerting their efforts to engage in the major battle, well demonstrates how fragmentary and ill-co-ordinated our wildlife policy is. In fact, the multiplicity of these agencies seems, more than anything else, to force us to ask – despite all assurances to the contrary – whether we truly have a wildlife policy at all.

This conflict of interest is to be found even in the public access policies of the Forestry Commission. The Commission has become increasingly aware of the wildlife resources of the forests and of the need for their conservation. In the early years of the Commission's existence rather too much attention seems to have been paid to preserving the habitat of the deer – very much to the exclusion of other forms of wildlife. In 1962, however, the Commission appointed its first wildlife officer and began to take a more rounded view of the wildlife on its lands. At the same time the policy of public access to large areas of Forestry-Commission land is at variance with the conservationists' concern to protect the habitat of wildlife, especially the rarer species, from intrusion. The Commission attempts to reconcile this by the creation of restricted Nature Reserves on its own property. It cannot be claimed to be a solution – but it is difficult to see how any other policy can be adopted.

It seems a rather unpalatable conclusion to reach – but it would appear that, unless we arrive at something approaching an environmental miracle, most of England's surviving native wildlife – and that of the rest of Britain for that matter – is doomed. And it is doomed largely because of the terrific expansion of population and of urban living. England's first major 'population explosion' of the late eighteenth and early nineteenth centuries did not threaten the countryside nearly so much because of the lack of transport facilities. Towns tended to be close-packed communities, the worker to live next-door to his factory. Today people can live forty or fifty miles from their place of work born thither along motorways or by commuter trains.

Urban expansion exists not merely to inflate vastly the perimeters of towns and cities but to quadruple the size of commuter villages, to push motorways across the country, to bring urbanization into the heart of the countryside, and because of the increasing pressures to produce intensive agriculture, to change the face of the countryside itself. Grain and feed silos are now only one of the more obvious changes as the countryside becomes a vast industry. To these may be added battery farming and the spreading modern version of the 'open field' system which is seeing the wholesale destruction of hedgerows, the latter often backed up with government subsidy. Hedgerow destruction ends the habitat of so much wildlife, while chemical pesticides can just as surely end its food supply.

At no other time has Robert Herrick's famous lines so applied to our countryside:

> Gather ye rosebuds while ye may
> For time it is a-flying
> And this same flower that blooms today
> Tomorrow will be dying.

What could once have been a fatalistic warning may very soon become an epitaph.

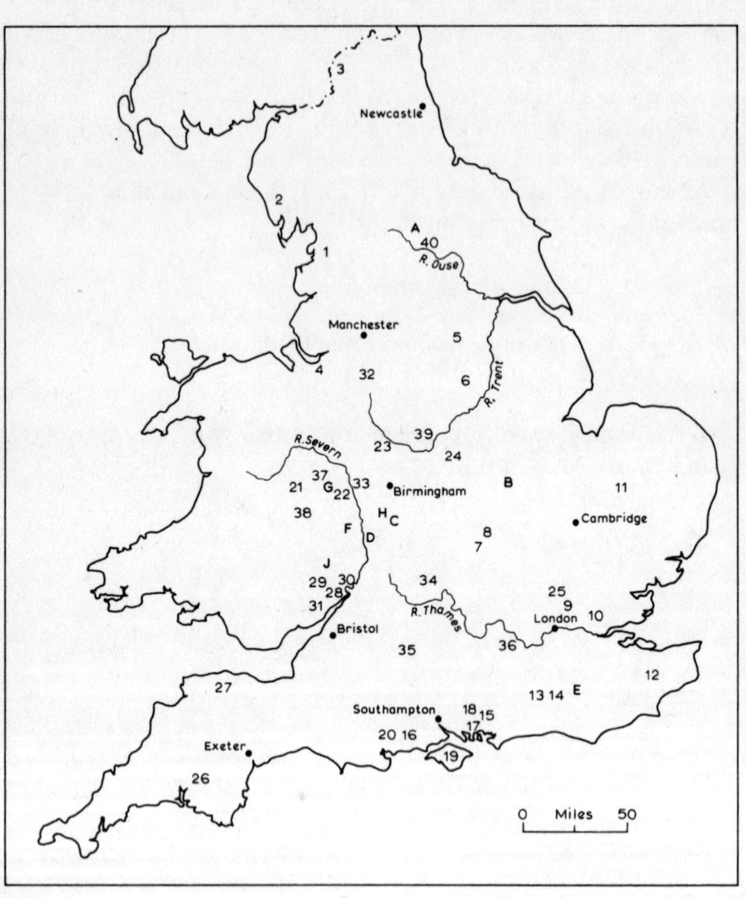
3
Newcastle
2
A
40
R. Ouse
1
Manchester
5
4
32
6
R. Trent
39
R. Severn
23
24
37
21
G
22
33
Birmingham
B
11
38
H
C
Cambridge
F
D
8
7
J
30
29
28
31
34
25
9
R. Thames
London
10
Bristol
36
35
12
27
13
14
E
Southampton
18
15
17
20
16
19
Exeter
26
0 Miles 50

Medieval Forsts –
now largely non-timbered

A KNARESBOROUGH
B ROCKINGHAM
C ARDEN
D HOREWELL
E THE WEALD
F MALVERN CHASE
G MORFE
H FECKENHAM
J CORSE

Modern Forestlands

1 Bowland
2 Hardknott Forest Park
3 Border National Forest Park
4 Delamere Forest
5 Derbyshire Woodlands
6 Sherwood Forest
7 Whittlewood Forest
8 Salcey Forest
9 Epping Forest
10 Hainault Forest
11 Breckland
12 Kent Woodlands
13 St Leonard's Forest
14 Ashdown Forest
15 Woolmer Forest
16 The New Forest
17 Bere Forest
18 Alice Holt Forest
19 Forest of Alvington
20 Cranbourne Chase
21 Clun Forest
22 Forest of Wyre – with Rock Forest
23 Cannock Chase
24 Charnwood Forest
25 Hatfield Forest
26 The Royal Forest of Dartmoor
27 Exmoor Forest
28 The Forest of Dean
29 The Highmeadow Woodlands
30 Dymock Forest
31 Wye Valley Woodlands – with Tintern Forest
32 Macclesfield Forest
33 Kinver Forest
34 Wychwood Forest
35 Savernake Forest
36 Windsor Great Forest
37 Wenlock Edge
38 Mortimer Forest
39 Needwood Forest
40 Fountains Abbey Woodlands

SELECT BIBLIOGRAPHY

Dartmoor – A New Study, ed. Crispin Gill, David & Charles, 1971

The Doomsday Geography of South-Western England – ed. H.C. Darby and R. Welldon Finn, Cambridge University Press, 1967

Immortal Sail, Henry Hughes, Stephenson & Co, Prescott, Lancs, 1969

Morfe Forest and Some of its People, W. Watlins-Pitchford, Journal Office, Bridgnorth, 1932

Easter And Its Customs, Christina Hole, Richard Bell, London, 1961

Woodland, J.D. Ovington, English University Press Ltd, 1965

Guide to British Hardwoods, W.P.B. Laidlaw, Leonard Hill (Books) Ltd, 1960

The Governance of Medieval England, H.G. Richardson and G.O. Sayles, 1963

Queen Elizabeth 1, J.E. Neale, Jonathan Cape, 1934

Cheshire 1630-1660, J.S. Merrill, Oxford University Press, 1974

Trees, Wood and Man, H.L. Eldin, Collins, 1970

A Documentary History of England, Vol 1, J.J. Bagley and P.B. Rowley, Penguin Books, 1966

Worcestershire, L.T.C. Rolt, Robert Hale & CO

Forest Service, George Ryle, David & Charles, 1969

The Peak District, K.C. Edwards, Collins, 1962

East And West of Severn, C.V. Hancock, Faber and Faber, 1956

Shrewsbury and Shropshire, Dorothy P.H. Wrenn, Longmans, 1968

The Midland Peasant, W.G. Hoskins, Macmillan, 1957

A Medieval Society, R.H. Hilton, Weidenfeld and Nicholson, 1966

The Challenge of Leisure, Michael Dower, The Civic Trust, 1965

Britain's National Parks, ed. H.L. Abrahams, Country Life Publications, 1959

British Woodland Trees, H.L. Eldin, Batsford, 1968

Portrait of Dartmoor, Vian Smith, Robert Hale & Co, 1966

Nicholl's Forest of Dean, H.G. Nicholls, David & Charles (Reprint), 1966

A Little History of Exmoor, Hope L. Bourne, Dent, 1968

The Cooper and His Trade, Kenneth Kilby, John Baker (Books) Ltd, 1971

Devon, W.G. Hoskins, Collins, 1954

Man, Nature and Ecology, J.A. Lauwerys, Joyce Joffe and A. Tucker, Aldus Books, 1974

Crossing's Hundred Years on Dartmoor, William Crossing, David and Charles (Reprint), 1967

Exmoor, S.H. Burton, Robert Hale & Co, 1974

Elizabethan Life in Town and Country, M. St Clare Byrne, Methuen, 1961

Forest Planning, D. Johnston, A.J. Grayson and R.J. Bradley, Faber & Faber, 1967

A Dictionary of British Folk Tales, Part B, Vols 1 and 2, Kathleen M. Briggs, Routledge & Kegan Paul, 1971

The King's War (1641-1647), C.V. Wedgwood, Collins

Trees, Gwen Allen & Joan Denslow, Oxford University Press, 1970

INDEX